Fifty Million *for* Faculty & Students

My Fundraising Years

Fifty Million *for* Faculty & Students

My Fundraising Years

ALICE LEE WILLIAMS BROWN

Fifty Million for Faculty & Students:
My Fundraising Years

Copyright © 2021 Alice Brown
All rights reserved.

No part of this publication may be reproduced, stored in a retrieval system or transmitted in any way by any means, electronic, mechanical, photocopy, recording or otherwise without the prior permission of the author except as provided by USA copyright law.

The opinions expressed by the author are not necessarily those of Wisdom House Books, Inc.

Published by Wisdom House Books, Inc.
Chapel Hill, North Carolina 27516 USA
1.919.883.4669 | www.wisdomhousebooks.com

Wisdom House Books is committed to excellence in the publishing industry.
Book design copyright © 2021 by Wisdom House Books, Inc. All rights reserved.
Cover and Interior Design by Ted Ruybal
Published in the United States of America

Paperback ISBN: 978-0-578-85781-7
LCCN: 2021908975

1. EDU013000 | EDUCATION / Finance
2. EDU015000 | EDUCATION / Higher
3. EDU050000 | EDUCATION / Collaborative & Team Teaching

First Edition

25 24 23 22 21 20 / 10 9 8 7 6 5 4 3 2 1

Dedication

This book is dedicated to Harry Neal Brown, my wonderful husband of over fifty years, who cooked dinner and raised our kids while I raised money and wrote this memoir—even though he is a better writer than I am and has published multiple books of poetry.

Table of Contents

Prologue. ix
How the History Became a Memoir 1
Relevant Personal Background 11
The Appalachian College Program (1980-1994) 19
    Background Informaiton. 19
    Working with Fellowship Recipients 23
    Staffing for the ACP 27
    Learning to Fundraise 28
    A Scholar Becomes an Administrator 33
    Formation of the Deans' Council .39
    Kentucky Elderhostel (Now Road Scholar) 40
    Restrictive Institutional Policies. .42
    Saving the ACP; Becoming the FSP (Faculty Scholars Program) 46
    Involving the Graduate Deans of the Regional Research Universities. 52
    Program Evaluation 56
    Efforts by UK to Keep the FSP. 58
    Leaving the University 60
The Appalachian College Association (1990-2008). 63
    Background 63
    Sunsetting FSP Initiatives 70
    Utilizing Task Forces 74
    Location and Staff in Berea 76
    The First Audit 79
    More about Staffing. 82

    New Facilities 93
    How to Become a President 97
    Strategic Plan 99
    Competition in Fundraising 105
    Sustaining Projects 109
    Building an Endowment for Fellowships and Grants 114
    Endowing Opportunities for Students 120
    Library Resources and Technology 134
    William G. Bowen Central Library of Appalachia 135
    Technology in Teaching 148
    Collaboration Across Colleges 164
    Summaries of Other Projects Funded between 1993-2008 168
    Another Strategic Plan 180

The Potential of Collaboration 189
    Building and Sustaining a Successful Consortium 194
    Closing a Consortium 213
    My Dream Consortium 216

Conclusion 219

Acknowledgements 221

Appendix A: Grants Written and Directed at ACA 1993-2008 225

Appendix B: Grants Received and Awards Made 1993-2008 229

Appendix C: Total Benefits Versus Dues Paid 1990-2008 257

About the Author 259

Prologue

Fundraising for Faculty and Students at Private Colleges: A Memoir

For almost forty years, as I have worked with multiple private colleges, I have watched strong colleges grow weak and weak colleges become strong. I have advised trustees at various colleges not to assume a new president will be the same as the past president. I have watched as new presidents remade colleges—some made the colleges better; some made unwise decisions that led to the decline of the institutions. In most cases, changes happen so gradually that within a few years no one remembers what the college once was: what its mission was, what had attracted students, what the campus had looked like, how successful the students were. Without knowledge of the past, there are few ways to determine if a college (or a program) is headed toward increasing success or decline.

One of my objectives for writing this book was to provide information about the development of a program initially funded by The Andrew W. Mellon Foundation to support faculty at thirty-five small private colleges in central Appalachia. From that one grant in 1979, many followed, providing additional opportunities for faculty and students with the average amount raised for the Appalachian College Program between 1979 and 1993 reaching roughly $3 million per year.[1] When the program became a nonprofit association, the annual awards increased.

Twenty major foundations and federal agencies provided support as the program grew from a base at the University of Kentucky (UK) into an independent association. This report provides historical information for the college presidents new to the Appalachian College Association (ACA) and for those presidents hoping to replicate the model established by it. Although the struggle of small private colleges in Appalachia is obvious, many similar colleges across the country, especially in other rural areas, are fighting (and praying) just as hard to continue their mission of providing the kind of education that best equips their students for a future of financial security and meaningful contributions.

Another objective was to illustrate the multiple benefits of collaboration across small private colleges and large public research universities. Too often, college presidents view other colleges as competition; and while they may not see major research universities as competition for their base of potential students, they may fail to see how working with faculty and staff at such large universities can be mutually beneficial.

When program officers from foundations that had supported the program at UK and the independent association read drafts of this document, they pointed out that an unanticipated benefit of writing it is the guidance provided for working with potential and existing funders.

---

1. It is important to note that the money raised throughout the first three decades (1979-2008) of the program/association was always focused on faculty and students, not on institutions. The belief was that strong faculty and special opportunities for students create strong colleges.

Prologue

The Appalachian College Association (ACA) began as the Appalachian College Program (ACP) based at the Appalachian Center at UK and offered its first fellowships for faculty from private colleges in central Appalachia in 1980. After roughly a decade, the program became the ACA, an independent 501 (c) (3) association housed in Berea, KY. That change was driven, in part, by the installation of a new president at UK who declared he could see no reason for a state university to host a program serving private colleges, only about a quarter of which were located in Kentucky. With support from most of the early funding sources, primarily The Andrew W. Mellon Foundation, the Pew Charitable Trusts, and the Exxon Education Foundation, the ACA established a home office in Berea, KY, and continued to attract funding from multiple sources to provide support and new opportunities for faculty and, beginning after the move to Berea, for students at the participating colleges.

By increasing resources for faculty to build on knowledge in their chosen disciplines and new pedagogies and by providing chances for students to participate in study abroad, service learning, and research experiences, the ACA has strengthened the participating institutions. This document provides the basis from which to evaluate the benefits and disadvantages of being housed within a research university and of establishing independent status as a non-profit association. It can assure the foundations, federal agencies, and individuals funding higher education that their dollars can make a difference in institutions struggling to improve the lives of those who choose to study and develop productive practices in the halls of the 1,687 private colleges and universities in the US. Almost half of those colleges and universities have fewer than 1,000 students[2], making them exceptionally vulnerable to closure. Program officers at foundations and federal agencies have proved time after time that they care about these small institutions in higher education and believe that by providing new opportunities for the faculty and students, they will strengthen the institutions as well as help those enrolled at those colleges and universities.

For the most part, this document reflects private foundations assisting private colleges. Such federal agencies as the National Science Foundation (NSF), the National Endowment for the Humanities (NEH), the Department of Education (DOE), and the Department of Commerce (DOC) all generously funded the ACA, but I was restricted by the presidents of the colleges served from contacting private individuals or companies who might be donors or potential donors for their institutions. Even a previous president of Berea College expressed concern that the foundations funding the ACA might think they were funding his college since the ACA offices were housed on the campus of that college. The fact was that Berea and perhaps Sewanee (University of the South) were among the few members of the ACA that had ever received funding, prior to the beginning of the ACA, from any of the foundations or federal agencies that gave generously to the ACA. What the ACP and ACA did was bring a lot of small colleges to the attention of a lot of nationally known funding sources. When the ACA needed matching funds for an NEH grant to endow the fellowships, library, and some of the ACA conferences, I did contact former fellowship recipients with the promise I would never ask them again for a contribution; about sixty percent gave.

---

2. Josh Moody, "A Guide to the Changing Numbers of US Universities," *US News* and *World Report*, Feb. 15, 2019.

Chapter 1

How the History Became a Memoir

Neither the decade of growth at UK nor the fifteen years I led the ACA at the new office in Berea have been documented with official histories.³ The program at UK and the association in Berea have supported faculty and students at over thirty private colleges across central Appalachia for over forty years. Still, many people, even the faculty and administrators at participating colleges, seem not to know how the ACA developed and what has been preserved from those early years. One reason for this lack of knowledge is the high rate of turnover among presidents at small colleges in rural areas; another is that there has been no official history of the first twenty-five years of the services provided—first by a program at UK and then as an independent non-profit association. Also, most small private college administrators tend to be cautious about opening their institutions to the public. As one president said, "We know we have problems; we just don't want everyone else to know about them." By not opening their colleges to the public, presidents hide their successes as well as their problems.

The ACA itself is difficult to define. Is the ACA a consortium? As it

---

3. Articles have been written about the ACA, but they have been based almost exclusively on interviews.

is currently constructed in the spring of 2021, ACA opportunities are driven by faculty from across the current thirty-five member colleges. The main office maintains a website which provides a variety of information about the work of the Association, but much of the information is accessible only by an "insider." There is little transparency; no longer is there a public annual report that is widely distributed. Today's ACA seems to be more like a consortium than an association dedicated to providing support for the individual faculty and students at member colleges.

As a consortium, the member colleges support each other; faculty serve as speakers and conveners; and membership dues cover administrative costs. Funding for fellowships and student grants and for the Bowen Central Library is drawn from interest on the endowment raised during the first twenty-five years of the development of the association. During those early years, with the support of over twenty foundations and federal agencies and many of the previous recipients of the benefits of the ACA, the ACA provided opportunities such as fellowships, grants, international studies, experiences in service learning, and assessments of learning outcomes. Assistance for faculty was determined by the needs faculty expressed; the applications were reviewed by a committee of six of the academic deans at the member colleges and six graduate deans (or their designees) from the research universities in the five-state region of central Appalachia—University of North Carolina at Chapel Hill, University of Virginia, Virginia Tech, University of Tennessee, West Virginia University, and University of Kentucky.

Early contributors to the ACP include The Andrew W. Mellon Foundation, the Pew Charitable Trusts, the Bingham Foundation, the Exxon Education Foundation, and the National Science Foundation, as well as multiple smaller foundations and federal agencies. Later, when the program became an independent association, additional funding came from the National Endowment for the Humanities (NEH), the Department of Commerce (DOC), the Berger Foundation, the Ledford Foundation, and the McCune Foundation—to mention those that gave the ACA from $500,000 to over $35 million. A look at the ACA when it was a nonprofit association funded by over twenty foundations, federal agencies, and many of the previous recipients will indicate why transparency was a critical element in the operations of the ACA: to maintain the continued financial support of funders from New York to California, it was necessary to maintain their trust. We were meticulous about reporting to those who provided the grants and gifts that helped faculty and, a bit later, students from the participating colleges. And, as one foundation officer said, "The ACA did more than they promised"; another said that the ACA could get more out of a dollar than any other organization he knew.[4]

After the program left UK and presidents of the participating colleges began to pay dues to cover major administrative costs, the ACA typically raised from $1 to $5 million per year for various services and opportunities for faculty and administrators from member colleges. One year the figure raised for such experiences was over $6 million.

Included in opportunities provided were the core opportunities that currently exist: fellowships and travel grants for faculty and research opportunities for students; participation in the online Central Library collections and advanced training for librarians; and two annual con-

---

4. Surely, the funders knew that holding workshops and other events in the region served (central Appalachia) costs much less than holding them in metropolitan areas—such as New York and Chicago.

ferences (the Summit, which began as the Technology Summit, and a summer Teaching and Learning Institute). Many of the opportunities funded between 1980 and 2008 by over seventy grants don't seem to exist today: international travel and study for faculty and students; internships for students pursuing degrees in medical sciences; training to qualify students to work as technology assistants; special experiences related to the arts in various forms (such as workshops in Pittsburgh, PA, hosted by the Pittsburgh Opera); research on the success of graduates from ACA colleges; funding for students to participate in service learning opportunities; and NSF scholarships for students.

Given the diversity of opportunities that developed, it seems important to trace the development of the ACA from its inception as the Appalachian College Program in 1980 until I retired in July of 2008. With encouragement from some early funders and new presidents at the member colleges, I decided to write that history.[5]

Unfortunately, I soon learned that even though an archivist had organized the many ACA records the year before my retirement, accessing historical information was problematic. The loss or misplacement of historical documents was attributed to the relocation of the central ACA office twice in the twelve years since my retirement and because the presidency of the organization had changed three times (with two separate years of leadership by an acting president). It was roughly six months after I requested copies of the annual reports of the ACA that had been produced during my tenure as ACA president before I received them. When the office could not locate an agreement for

---

5. Several years after I retired, the new director of the Appalachian Center at UK called me to learn about the ACP which led to the development of the ACA. She indicated that she wished there were a history of the Appalachian Center itself.

the endowment established roughly five years before my retirement, I realized that writing a history based on official records would prove difficult, if not impossible. As a result, the history I intended to write was discarded in favor of writing a memoir. While I had not taken any official ACA documents when I retired, I had a few personal calendars and some barely legible notes; I had assumed that if I needed more, I could request whatever I needed, and it would be readily available. Since that was not the case, I realized that all I could write was what I remembered, recognizing that my personal remembrances may or may not be completely accurate without the opportunity to review historical documentation, and the history of the ACA became a memoir.

I am setting forth my memories to the best of my ability, which does not mean my memories are either entirely accurate or complete.

When I retired from the ACA in 2008, every other employee who had been working there left within a year of my departure—except an employee in the Bowen Central Library who had been there only a few years. As a result, there was no person with the institutional history of the Association who could explain how the ACA developed and operated between 1980 until 2008. There has always been a lot of turnover among presidents of the member colleges, and even the few long-term leaders have had little time to devote to remembering or recording the history of the ACA. At the time of this writing—just over a decade after I was named President Emerita of the ACA—only six of the numerous presidents I once served were still at ACA colleges: Bill Luckey at Lindsey Wilson (KY); Mike Carter at Campbellsville (KY); Joe Stepp at Alice Lloyd (KY); Paul Conn at Lee (TN); David Olive at Bluefield (VA); and David Joyce at Union (KY) and now at Brevard (NC). They are the ones most likely to be able to judge the accuracy of this document.

Some of this information was reported by Leila Weinstein in her article "Appalachian College Association History," May 2008, prepared for distribution at my retirement dinner. She interviewed twenty people from foundations and the colleges served and described the ACA as "strong, sustainable, and dedicated to its member institutions." Also useful is an article written by Stephanie Roark Keener: "Core Resources, These Appalachian Colleges: An Interview with Alice Brown," *Appalachian Journal: A Regional Studies Review*, Appalachian State University, Vol. 36, Numbers 1-2, Fall 2008/Winter 2009, pp.54-85. What is here in this memoir that is not in those documents is more insight into the difficulties and the triumphs the ACA encountered between 1980 and 2008.

In 2000, a new president at one of the member colleges mentioned at his first ACA meeting that he did not understand the ACA. When a representative from The Mellon Foundation who was visiting mentioned that the ACA website contained a lot of information, his reply was, "Information? I don't need information!" Then he held up the package of information sent to him by the ACA office for that meeting. He continued, "I have information; what I don't have is understanding." While a history of the ACA would provide information, a memoir might provide more understanding.

Since the primary target population for this memoir is the presidents and academic deans of the colleges who are members of the ACA, my goal is to provide some understanding of how one grant from one foundation grew to over forty grants from over twenty funders and the benefits derived from the over $50 million raised. The policies and practices that enabled me and a couple of staff members (none of whom had held a position requiring them to write grants prior to working at the ACA) should be helpful to deans and presidents at other small colleges as well.

What is contained here are conversations and incidents that occurred in the first twenty-five years of the ACA development—as it grew from being the Appalachian College Program (a funded project housed at the Appalachian Center at UK) to being a program of the UK Graduate School (known as the Faculty Scholars Program) to being an independent 501(c)(3) association housed in Berea, KY—the Appalachian College Association. By the time I retired, the ACA had slightly less than $25 million in endowment funds, over $3 million in grants for existing projects, and about $250,000 in reserve funds.

Comments in quotation marks indicate what I remember was said, not necessarily the exact quote. Stories inserted as footnotes simply help in understanding the spirit that existed at different times. I have taken the liberty to spell out names of people, states, and colleges only when it is important to do so for clarity. For example, I may refer to Dr. William G. Bowen, the president of The Mellon Foundation (during most of the years I was at the ACA) and the president of Princeton University before Mellon, as Dr. Bowen or as Bill when it is clear to whom I am referring.

To clarify what might result in confusion as you read this memoir, the program being described was initially established as the Appalachian College Program (ACP) based at the Appalachian Center at the University of Kentucky (UK); then it was moved to the Graduate School at UK and became the Faculty Scholars Program (FSP); then it became a nonprofit association housed first at Warren Wilson

College in NC and then moved to an office in Berea, KY—the Appalachian College Association (ACA). All three—the ACP, FSP, and ACA—were basically the same program.

A *Chronicle of Higher Education* article by Lawrence Biemiller (March 27, 2016) is entitled "The Truth-Teller: Once a Small-College Champion, Now a Tough Critic." This memoir is my effort to tell the truth, based on my memories, a few bits of information from old calendars, and annual ACA reports produced during my tenure at the ACA. However, others may remember events differently than the way I have described them. I welcome information indicating major errors or contradictory memories or differences of opinion. I am only setting forth my memories to the best of my ability, which does not mean my memories are either entirely accurate or complete. One person who read early drafts sent me a note indicating his memory was not what mine was about his experiences at the ACA. He was kind enough to add that this memoir is my memories, not his, and my memories present him more favorably than those of one of the former staff members at the ACA. What I would really welcome is for some scholar to write a dissertation or history of the ACA, tracing its development back from inception until a recent date—someone who could search archives of the Appalachian Center at UK and other records that might be stored at UK or in other offices as well as the archives of the ACA—wherever they may be.

This document is divided into four major sections: my Personal Background, the History of the Appalachian College Program (including the history of the Faculty Scholars Program), the History of the Appalachian College Association, and my observations about the potential of collaboration. The narrative is followed by Acknowledgements and three

Appendices: (A) Grants Written and Directed 1993-2008; (B) Awards Made Between 1993-2008 (as reflected by annual reports); and (C) Benefits vs. Dues 1990-2008 (indicating the benefits each college received and the dues each paid).

I hope readers will know when they finish this memoir that (1) there are multiple benefits to be derived from collaboration, especially in collaborating to raise money that can benefit multiple colleges; (2) when public and private colleges collaborate, the best of both can benefit each participating institution; (3) presidents who refuse to collaborate because they think weaker colleges will hinder their progress might find that helping their weaker brother and sister institutions can benefit their own colleges more than expected; (4) greed seldom benefits any individual or institution; and (5) there are multiple charitable foundations and even some federal agencies that are anxious to help those who clearly need and appreciate their help.

Chapter 2

Relevant Personal Background

I understand that in writing a memoir, I should begin with information about my background that led to my becoming the director of the Appalachian College Program (ACP) at UK and then president of the Appalachian College Association (ACA) based in Berea, KY.

Shortly before my birth, Pearl Harbor was bombed. I was born in my father's hometown (Statesville, NC), but we soon moved to Baltimore, MD, where my father worked at the Glenn L. Martin airplane factory and looked after me while my mother worked at night as a waitress. After the war, my father took courses in installing automobile glass and repairing appliances in Chicago, IL, while my mother and I lived in Todd, NC, with her mother. To this day, Todd remains fairly isolated on Three Top Mountain near Boone, and we lived the life my mother had known as a child. We canned apples, carried water from a nearby spring, used an outhouse, took sponge baths or played in the creek nearby, and listened to the snakes and rats racing between the walls as we lay awake at night.[6]

---

[6]. I once offered an impressive physics professor a job just after he learned he had not gotten tenure at the ACA college where he was teaching. He had led several ACA workshops; the Mellon folks were as impressed with him as I was. I offered him a job at the ACA, which he turned down, saying, "I don't think you live the Appalachian culture; I don't know if you admire it, but you understand it. I could never understand it."

Fifty Million *for* Faculty & Students: *My Fundraising Years*

When my father returned from Chicago, we moved from my grandmother's house to the home of two of my aunts in Statesville, NC, while my parents bought and operated a service station-grocery store[7] on Boulevard, a wide street in a residential area. After a year or so of sharing a small house with my grandfather and aunts, my parents built a house near the station. I must have been able to walk to Avery Sherill School because I don't remember ever being driven to school. My first-grade teacher had been my father's first-grade teacher.

When I was in the fifth grade, my parents sold the service station-grocery store to one of my aunts and bought a farm about ten miles away in Troutman. Charlotte was about forty miles away, but it could have been 400 miles away given the fact that the only time we traveled there was for a medical matter.

My mother restored the farmhouse, and my father built a new service station (and glass shop) about a mile from the farm. With forty acres of land, a dozen or so cattle, two large chicken houses (where we raised the chickens that produced the hundreds of eggs I "candled"[8] and my parents sold), and a service station with a few groceries and glass shop to operate, my parents worked from 7 a.m. until 9 p.m. six days a week. I never knew them to take a vacation (or go to church except on Easter and Christmas), but they sent me to church with

---

7. Today our service station-grocery store might be called a "convenience store;" but our store was primary a service station, where my father pumped gas, changed oil and tires, fixed automobile glass, and made minor repairs on vehicles. Groceries were on a few shelves in the back of the store and in a large cooler. I spent lots of time building forts from empty boxes, reading comic books sold in the store, and eating Vienna sausages.

8. No, I didn't mean "handled" the eggs; they were "candled" by holding them up to a light to determine if they were fresh. We were selling eggs and wanted to be sure they did not have large air sacs, indicating they were no longer fresh; those wanting their eggs to hatch candled them to watch the growth of the embryos.

my aunts and on a couple of excursions with other relatives. By the time of this move, I had a brother who was seven. I suppose he was never old enough to travel away from home before vacations became a thing of the past for all my family. We did travel to Todd, NC, near Boone at least once a month to take groceries and cut wood for my grandmother. My brother and I played in the creek nearby while the water cooled the melons we had brought with us; then we had a picnic. Those visits were our vacations.

Troutman was a typical county school (grades 1-12 in two buildings—probably about 500 students). By the tenth grade, I was playing basketball and marching as a majorette, as well as maintaining about a 4.0 GPA (at least I don't remember ever making a B). I was also taking care of the station while my mother was helping at the former station and my father was working in hay or doing some other farm chore. (Fortunately, we never had a garden, but I did help vaccinate a lot of chickens.) As at other small schools, the principal (Mr. Sinclair) knew every student and his/her parents; he often came to my class to tell me I needed to drive home; the cattle were out. I had a car just for such occasions, and it didn't matter if I were in the middle of taking a test, I could go home and come back to finish the test as soon as I could. And Mr. Sinclair knew which students were going to Appalachian State Teachers' College (ASTC)—now Appalachian State University (ASU); he had taken most of them to the college to register and help them with financial aid. As one alumnus from Troutman said, "Mr. Sinclair knew I was going to college before my parents did." He had also bought gym clothes for students who could not afford them.

I had known I was going to ASTC since I was old enough to know what a college was. ASTC was near my mother's homeplace, and it was probably the only college she knew. It was, in fact, the school her mother had attended when it was a normal school, long enough to qualify to teach in a one-room school near her house. Neither my mother nor my father had gone to college; Mother attended school until about the eighth grade—as high a grade as the school nearby offered. My father had quit school when he was about eleven years old; as the youngest of twelve children, he had lots of brothers and sisters to teach him. He spent the years he might have been in high school and college as an itinerant farm worker traveling across the country, following produce that needed harvesting.

From fifth grade (when my family moved to Troutman) through the eighth grade, it seems that the only aspect of my education that was a bit unusual was the practice of memorizing Bible verses. After learning a certain number, each student got a free week at a summer camp—where we learned more Bible verses.

In the ninth grade, students who had attended elementary school at a nearby orphanage (Barium Springs) started attending Troutman High. Suddenly, there were a lot of good-looking new guys to date; the Barium boys were the best football and basketball players, if not the best scholars. My tenth-grade boyfriend did, however, get taken from Troutman in the eleventh grade to attend a prep school (Phillips Exeter Academy), based, I assume, on his high scores on standardized tests. (I still have his Phillips Exeter pin.) And all students from Barium had the option of attending a college of their choice—if they could get admitted—and most did. Our graduating class was about thirty boys and thirty girls. Those who were not married by the end of the summer or had not joined the army after graduation went to college. I was fortunate to have been born near Appalachia but not deep within it and to a mother who had grown up near a college and a father who was not opposed to higher education, although none of his eleven siblings seem to have ever even considered attending college.

I was also lucky to have attended a rural public school where students were encouraged to go to college. A few of us worked at the local shirt factory the summer we graduated from high school and knew we had made the right decision—to go to college. According to 2012 data, while thirty percent of working age adults in the U.S. had at least a bachelor's degree, in central Appalachia, only thirteen percent had a degree. In fact, in central Appalachia, where educational statistics are the most dire, twenty percent of working-age adults lacked a high school diploma, and half of those counties where poverty levels were below the U.S. rate ($22,113 for a family of four) were in the central region of Appalachia, where the unemployment rate was ten percent, with the national rate being six point four percent.[9]

Most graduates of Troutman High School, like me, went to ASTC—where scholarships were available for those promising to teach in a NC public school for two years after graduation. None of the boys from Barium went to Appalachian; I assume they went to Presbyterian private colleges tuition-free. When I learned that several of the Barium boys were going to the University of North Carolina (UNC) as juniors, I told my father I wanted to transfer from Appalachian. He dismissed that idea by asking why he should pay $1,200 instead of $600 in tuition. Fortunately, my senior year at Appalachian, I met my future husband, who had graduated from Davidson and was working

---

9. Data is from a March 2012 article by Paola Scommegna at the Population Reference Bureau. It is important to remember that this data is fairly recent. The public school and college graduation rates in the late 1950s would have been much lower.

on his master's degree at Appalachian. I could quit thinking about the boys from Barium.

Beginning in high school, I had mentors who steered me in the right direction. In high school, Miss Godfrey, the girls' basketball coach, kept me on track to college for four years. In college, Cratis Williams, the Appalachian scholar known to practically everyone who has ever taken a course in Appalachian studies, was the professor for many of the courses I took. The year I graduated, he was dean of the Graduate School, and he offered me an assistantship working in his office. I had finished the undergraduate degree in English in three years, and I was ready to leave college. I rejected Dr. Williams' offer—probably one of my first "great mistakes"—and found a job teaching English and coaching the girls' basketball team at Cary High School in NC.

Cary, NC, was near my soon-to-be-husband's hometown; and he was stationed at Fort Bragg, fulfilling his obligation as an ROTC student. After we married, I moved to Fort Bragg and taught there for a year before we moved to Banner Elk, where my husband had a job at Lees-McRae, then a two-year college, and I went to Appalachian for my M.A. in English. When my degree was completed, I taught full-time as an instructor at Appalachian until we moved to Athens, Ohio, so my husband could work on his doctorate and I could teach part-time for the first year and full-time the next two years. Ohio University (OU) loved hiring wives of students; there was not much of a possibility we would stay long enough to seek tenure. After our first year at OU, we returned to NC for the summer of 1968 so I could have our son at the UNC Medical Center. After another year at OU, with his Ph.D. almost in hand, my husband accepted a position at Eastern KY University (EKU), and I taught at Madison Central High School for almost a year. That spring, I had our daughter and began teaching part-time at EKU. I worked for a while as an instructor in the Learning Lab at Eastern, and then took a leave to accept an assistantship and complete my doctorate at UK.

After finishing at UK, I returned to EKU to work as a conference planner in a new office established to offer non-credit courses and special programs, which later included the state Elderhostel program (now called Road Scholar).[10] Several years after setting up non-credit courses (such as basket making, cake decorating, and swimming) and hosting conferences for groups across the nation, Ramona Lumpkin (whom I had met at a conference for directors of continuing education programs) called and told me there was an opening in a similar office at UK. About three months after I started working in the Office of Conferences and Institutes at UK, I received a call from a different office at UK—the Appalachian Center. John Stephenson was director of the Center.

John had once taught at Lees-McRae, and we had met on several occasions—such as the time we were on the same flight from D.C., and when we arrived in Lexington, his wife was waiting with his children and my husband was waiting with ours.[11] When he called me, John had just accepted the presidency at Berea College; he needed to fill a vacancy in the Center before he left. The director of the

---

10. Elderhostel, when I was state director for Kentucky, was a national non-profit which provided educational programs for people over fifty. Programs were usually held on college campuses, where participants stayed in dorms and ate in dining halls; regular professors from the campus taught three academic courses and the Elderhostel coordinator arranged field trips relevant to the subjects taught. Today, the program is called Road Scholar and is international in scope; participants now typically stay and dine in hotels near college campuses.

11. I noticed our daughter (about two years old) had her dress on backward; apparently my husband had not noticed. Still, when my children grew up, they frequently reminded me about what a good father they had.

Appalachian College Program (Ramona Lumpkin) had just left to be the new director of the Kentucky Humanities Council. As a new employee at UK, I could not transfer to a new position until I had been at the University for at least six months, but John agreed to hold the position for the time remaining for me to fulfill the six months required before transferring to the Appalachian Center. I was hired to work in the Center directing a program funded in 1979 by The Andrew Mellon Foundation—the Appalachian College Program, and I moved to the Center in the summer of 1983.

Chapter 3

The Appalachian College Program (1980-1994)

Background Information

Many times, I heard the story about how the Appalachian College Program (ACP) was conceived and secured at UK. In 1979, John Stephenson visited Claire List at The Andrew W. Mellon Foundation. He had gone to NY to seek funding for the new Appalachian Center at UK. Claire informed him that the Foundation did not fund centers; the only priority for the Foundation at that time was supporting humanities faculty engaged in academic research. John immediately recognized an opportunity for the UK Appalachian Center and asked if Mellon would provide fellowships for humanities faculty from private colleges in central Appalachia to come to UK during the summer months to conduct research in their disciplines. John had received his Ph.D. in Sociology at UNC-Chapel Hill and taught at Lees-McRae College, where he found that being the only sociologist at a small two-year college in the North Carolina mountains was rewarding, but not having colleagues with a major interest in his academic field or access to a major research library was frustrating. John's request at Mellon resulted in a three-year grant of $280,000, with the stipulation that funding awarded and all interest earned would be used to provide the fellowships and related administrative salaries, not for overhead expenses at UK. He was pleasantly surprised to learn that grants funded by Mellon were paid "up front," and UK was not allowed to take any of the interest earned. The original $280,000 would earn enough interest for him to hire a full-time director of the program, not the part-time one he had anticipated.

To understand my strong focus on academic content instead of on pedagogy throughout my career, it is worth noting that when the first director of the Appalachian College Program (ACP) attracted the attention of the Foundation program officer (Claire List), she contacted John to make it clear that Mellon did not provide funding to help ACA faculty with issues related to pedagogy; what Mellon was interested in was helping faculty improve their academic expertise. They were happy to see the fellowships awarded; they were not happy that Mellon money had been used to support a conference on pedagogy. I learned not to use the word "conference" in communicating with Mellon; to the board there, "conference" was just another word for "party." I was to talk about institutes, symposia, or seminars.[12] Mike Nichols, that first director of the ACP, resigned, and Ramona Lumpkin became the second director of the ACP.

Ramona and her assistant did an amazing job of developing the ACP, keeping meticulous records and impressing Mellon. She directed the Program until 1984 when John became president of Berea College and she became director of the Kentucky Humanities Council. I was working in the Division of Conferences and Institutes at UK when

---

12. Later, at UK I learned to avoid certain words when requesting reimbursements; a celebration was "an official University function."

John called and said that the search for a new director of the ACP had not produced a candidate the Appalachian Center search committee would approve; then he asked if I would apply for the position if the search was reopened. Jim Hougland from the Sociology Department became acting director of the Center about the time I moved to my new office in a large old house just up the hill from the Appalachian Center. Jim explained that I was hired because I could "operate with a great deal of autonomy," and the director of the Appalachian Center would have multiple other responsibilities that would take his time.[13]

Even after I graduated from college, I had numerous mentors. Earl Wallace had grown up in Appalachian Kentucky, attended UK and spent most of his life working at Standard Oil and in the investment banking firm of Dillon and Reed. After retirement, he led the campaign to restore Shaker Village of Pleasant Hill in KY and served as a personal adviser to me, helping raise the fellowship endowment at UK. Certainly, John Stephenson and Jim Hougland and numerous professors at UK opened doors to multiple opportunities for me. But it was Alice (Tish) Emerson, my program officer at Mellon, and Bill Bowen, the president at The Mellon Foundation, who provided the most opportunities for me after I became the director of the Appalachian College Program. Even after I retired, Dr. Bowen stayed in touch; he wrote the foreword for one of my first books (*Cautionary Tales*) and recruited me for a study of Sweet Briar College during the year the college almost closed.

Tish once told me that one reason the board at Mellon was interested in continuing to fund the Appalachian College Program was because

---

13. As I will point out later, the new director who arrived the next year did not want me to be autonomous.

Jack Sawyer, just before he retired as president of the Foundation, told the board that he hoped they would continue to fund the ACP, expressing his admiration for the mission and success of the program. In the "Appalachian College Association History" that Leila Weinstein wrote, she quoted Bill Bowen as suggesting that one reason for Mellon's strong support of education in Appalachia probably stems from the family's connections to the coal in Appalachia:

> The Mellon Foundation has a long history of involvement with the Appalachian colleges, going back, I think, to the activities of the Mellon family in Pennsylvania and throughout Appalachia. They were very much involved in industrial projects in and around Pittsburgh in coal mining and so forth.... I presume they felt that having been economically so involved with Appalachia and the areas around Appalachia, that it just made sense for the Foundation to provide some support to the indigenous institutions of the area. They must have felt that it was a right thing to do (p.12).

Leila wrote that the relationship between the ACA and The Mellon Foundation developed into one of trust where Mellon did not simply respond to requests from the ACA, Mellon "actually engaged itself in thinking about ways it could be useful to the ACA" (p. 12). She quoted Tish Emerson:[14] "We tried to understand what the opportunities and needs were for this group of colleges and then tried to think of ways we could be helpful" (p. 13).

---

14. Tish had served as president of Wheaton College in Norton, MA, for sixteen years before joining the staff at Mellon, so her interest in private colleges was understandable.

Working with Fellowship Recipients

Recipients of the Mellon fellowships were initially chosen by the chairs of the humanities divisions; later, when Pew funded fellowships for faculty in the sciences, chairs of the math and science divisions joined those from the humanities on the fellowship review committee.

Funding required the fellows to come to UK, have office space in the building of the ACP or, after Pew provided fellowships for faculty in math and science, in an appropriate science lab, and use the University library and other resources to complete (or at least make progress on) a research project. The ACP staff helped fellows locate housing in Lexington; generally, there were houses UK faculty vacated during sabbaticals and the fellows could rent those or ones commercially available. Each fellow had a UK mentor (unpaid) in his or her discipline; the mentor's responsibility was to talk with the fellow about his/her research and to let me know if there were problems related to the progress of the project. Each week of the summer sessions, the fellows met for a brown-bag lunch on the front porch of our building to share their research results with each other and any UK faculty who wished to attend.[15]

Periodically, we had speakers present talks on such subjects as the relationship between the sciences and humanities. We had picnics where fellows brought their families. The fellowships were named to honor James Still, a highly regarded writer living in eastern KY; we

---

15. I grew concerned that topics presented by science faculty were unrelated to the interests of the humanities faculty. I thought we should have different days in the week for the humanities and science presentations. There was an outcry by the humanities faculty who said listening to the research of the science fellows made them acutely aware of how difficult it must be to teach such content to students at their colleges.

celebrated his birthday every year. One fellow told me that I would make a great Boy Scout leader.

During the academic year, the ACP hosted seminars on topics such as critical thinking, and faculty in arts and sciences disciplines from all the participating colleges were invited to attend. I was repeatedly surprised by the willingness of well-known scholars to travel to UK to make a presentation for an honorarium of $100. For example, when I called Robin Lovin, noted for his study of Reinhold Niebuhr and the intersection of religion and politics, he said he would be delighted to come to an ACP event as the major speaker, and that since he was scheduled to make a presentation in NC the day before the date of the ACP event, he would just charge the ACP for the cost of the stopover in Lexington on his way home. Later, when UK heard about his presentation with the ACP and called to ask Lovin to speak at a workshop hosted by the University, Lovin charged several thousand dollars.

There were many other cases where talented people would help the ACP for little or no stipend. When David Baldacci spoke at a meeting of the ACA college presidents, his foundation gave the ACA $5,000.[16] Such people found it easy to give to a program that supported those sharing their expertise to help disadvantaged students across a region of poverty escape that deprivation, get a good education, and find meaningful and rewarding work. It is easy to justify helping a program that gives students in such a region significant educational experiences beyond those their colleges can afford to provide.

We had money for faculty to travel to professional seminars to make

---

16. Another speaker began his presentation by saying, "Alice called and asked me if I believed in free speech. I said that I did. She said, 'That's good because I want you to give one.'"

presentations in their disciplines, and we had funding for Traveling Scholars—UK faculty who would travel to an ACP college and make a presentation at a convocation or seminar. If the colleges selected were a long distance from Lexington, the Traveling Scholar would often make the presentation at several colleges that were geographically close to each other. Examples of topics presented follow: Ray Betts (Honors Program) "Heroes and Heroism"; Dwight Billings (Sociology) "Religion and Politics"; George Herring (History) multiple presentations about the war in Vietnam; Charles Elton (Higher Education) "Trends in Higher Education"; Wendell Berry (English) readings from his poetry and fiction; and Eric Christianson (History) "Role of Science in a Democratic Society." We paid each Traveling Scholar $100 a presentation, regardless of his or her credentials, and mileage and per diem for overnight travel.

Ray Betts, head of UK's honors program, was active in the ACP. He held receptions for fellowship recipients at the Honors House and was a popular speaker. Once when I called to ask if he would make a presentation at Union College (in eastern KY), he said that he was tired of going to a college for an hour or so, that he wanted to "take over" a college for a weekend. He suggested French Impressionism as the focus for multiple presentations—the art, literature, and theatre, as well as the history, of that period. The reaction of the academic dean at Union was that there would be little interest in such a topic for students from rural Kentucky. Betts then suggested, since it was 1986—the 100th anniversary of the first gasoline-powered automobile—the topic could center on automobiles. The chair of the UK Art Department spoke about how art in the late 1800s influenced the design of cars. The chair of the UK Theatre Department wrote a play about the life of Henry Ford; it was performed twice at Union (once for public school students and again in the evening for the college students and general public). He also taught a workshop on "From Page to Stage" for the Union students. The chair of Geography at UK spoke about how the growth of cities impacted the development of automobile travel. And Betts talked about the automobile in movies. He arranged for a display of antique cars to be held at Union,[17] and students at the college arranged an exhibit of family photographs of old cars.

In addition to serving as Traveling Scholars, UK faculty visited ACP colleges to serve as outside evaluators for students being considered for special recognition; the fellowship recipients often received equipment that the University had declared surplus but was valuable for the fellows' research; faculty at UK praised the work of the fellows and the fact that they were telling graduate students at UK what it was like to teach in a small college. In short, the connections between UK and the colleges strengthened every year from 1980 until 1993.

For a while, funding was available to name an outstanding faculty member from one of the ACA colleges. This award was dropped when the UK committee choosing the winner of the cash award concluded that all that was being accomplished was giving another award to faculty who had already received similar awards. Also, early in the development of the ACP, funding was available for scholars from universities outside UK to come to UK to study topics related to Appalachia—one came from Cornell; another from the University of Tennessee; another from Wales; and another from Italy.

---

17. Betts invited Paul Newman to bring a car—an invitation which Newman never acknowledged.

Staffing for the ACP

I had several secretaries in the ten years I worked at the Appalachian Center. The first I inherited from the previous director of the ACP; the second was Pat Smith, who had worked at UK in earlier years and returned about the time I was looking for assistance; the third was Eugene Zita, at that time more knowledgeable about computer technology than anyone else in the office. All were amazingly competent and dedicated.

When I asked for additional help, Dan Reedy, dean of the Graduate School and a member of the committee for reviewing fellowship applications, said, "Get a graduate student from Library Science; they're very organized." I did and she was. Robin Weinstein was quiet but committed to her assignments. When I left to establish an office in Berea, it was Robin who knew enough about all aspects of the UK program to be able to phase it out with a great deal of efficiency.

Then Reedy himself said we needed at least a half-time accountant; all our financial operations went through his office and the load was beginning to create more work than his staff could handle.

We hired a woman who had worked in accounting at other UK offices. Her first complaint was that she did not have adequate equipment; we got her a new computer and printer. Next, she complained about sharing an office; we moved everyone else around to give her a private office. Then she complained about being half-time, not having enough time to do the work; we made her full-time. Then it became clear that the work was beyond her competency level. When I went to Dean Reedy and said that I had made a mistake in hiring her and needed to fire her, his response was, "You hired her; you have to work with her." He explained how difficult it was to fire anyone at UK, given the long process of evaluations, warnings, and then termination. I could not claim "financial exigency," requiring a reduction in staff, since it was clear we needed an accountant; our outside funding was increasing quarterly. The fact that I could not fire an employee helped later in my decision to leave UK.

Despite the relatively small staff, one agenda for a staff meeting read: plans for March seminars; plans for an institute in mid-June; plans for review of fellowship applications; development of proposals for new grants; discussions with Jim Rogers, chair of the Theatre Department, related to a performance of James Still stories. The variety of services provided by the ACP to benefit faculty at colleges in central Appalachia increased each year.

Learning to Fundraise

When I became director of the ACP, Stephenson had just received the second grant from Mellon to continue the fellowships for humanities faculty. As he was leaving UK to become president at Berea College, he told me that I should apply to the Pew Charitable Trusts for funding for science faculty; he had been contacted by Pew staff about their new interest in funding colleges in Appalachia. While Pew's interest at the time was related to helping colleges upgrade physical facilities, such as libraries, John thought they might fund the ACP to provide fellowships for faculty in the sciences. I invited all the chairs of the UK undergraduate science departments to meet with me to discuss what should be included in such a proposal. Their first suggestion was to request money for year-long fellowships. Science research is not like that in the humanities, they pointed out. Science faculty need labs and equipment, not just books. The outline for the proposal included grants of up to $30,000 for faculty to spend an academic year working in a UK lab on a project chosen by the fellowship recipient. When that proposal was funded and applications began to arrive, the chairs of the science departments joined the chairs of the humanities departments as the committee selecting fellowship recipients.

When I sent a draft of the Pew proposal to the chair of the Physics Department, he sent it back saying, "This reads like a speech for Jessie Jackson; get all this emotional stuff out and just give Pew the facts." Later, when I wrote a proposal for the Mary Reynolds Babcock Foundation, the director there called me and said, "My Board wants to weep when they read; if this is important to you, put some emotion in it." Thus, my first lesson in fundraising was that each funder has not just guidelines but also preferences regarding how a request should be presented. The secret is to find out what the funding source wants to encourage and what attracts the potential contributor's attention long enough for you to build a case for your project. The best way to learn that is to visit or at least call the funding agency. As Robert Zemsky, a well-known faculty member, speaker, and consultant from the University of Pennsylvania, cautioned: "If something is important to you, you should communicate about it face-to-face or at least voice-to-voice. Letters and emails are too easily ignored."

On a trip to New York to meet with program officers at the Open Society Foundation and Ilene Mack at the Hearst Foundation, the lesson about learning what funders expect was again illustrated. I met with a program officer at the Open Society, started talking about the ACA and was stopped by the foundation's representative telling me they did not give grants to organizations, only to individuals. (Later, a representative did tour some of the ACA colleges with me and talked with various faculty, but I do not think any ever received a grant from the Open Society.)

Then, on my way to see Ilene Mack at Hearst, I reviewed information about what Hearst funds. As soon as I sat down in Ilene's office, I started by saying, "I know that Hearst is especially interested in nursing programs." Ilene said, "I know what we fund; what do you need us to fund?" Not only did we get a series of endowment gifts from Hearst, but Ilene also invited Ligia Cravo at the Foundation to meet with me on several occasions—giving me access to a Hearst program officer after Ilene retired—though after she retired, I often spent the night at Ilene's apartment in New York when I was fundraising in the city, so our friendship extended past the time of our professional relationship until her death in 2013. She took me to multiple plays and performances in New York, trying to expose me to a culture I had not known much about.

I have remained in contact with many of the program officers I worked with during my tenure at the ACA. To this day, Martha Perry, my program officer at the McCune Foundation in Pittsburgh, visits me; she is retired and lives in VA, about a two-hour drive from my home in NC. I talk with various people who work or did work at Mellon when I was at the ACA. My program officer at Exxon, Dick Johnson, and his wife, Novella, visited from Minnesota on several occasions after I had retired. And I could list those at NEH and NSF that I remained in touch with for several years after I retired—and before they retired.[18]

---

18. I once tried to reach Duncan McBride, who had become my contact at NSF after Robert Watson left his position there. After a number of unsuccessful attempts, I called his assistant and asked if he had left NSF. She said, "No, he is here," and transferred me to him. "Duncan," I said, "when I can't reach you, at my age all I can assume is that you died." He laughed and said, "No, I've just been really busy." These connections with funding sources served me well after I retired when I consulted for several colleges about fundraising and several foundations funded research for the books I have written.

A proposal submitted to the Exxon Education Foundation by John Stephenson before he left UK had been returned prior to review with a recommendation that the budget be cut to below $100,000. At that level, staff could approve the award without review by the Exxon board. (Another lesson learned was that it is not unusual for large foundations to have a policy for allowing program staff to make grants of small amounts without a review by the board of the foundation.) Once I resubmitted the proposal to Exxon, the ACP received $92,000 for preparing faculty and staff to use technology. At that time, most of the workshops funded were related to the creation of Word documents and most attending were staff, not faculty. Later, Exxon gave the ACP $10,000 to host a conference for the academic deans. Those early grants from Exxon led to multiple other benefits of our affiliation with that foundation and the program officer there.[19]

During a recent move, I found a note saying that the year Jim Hougland was acting director of the Appalachian Center, I wrote seven proposals, and they were all funded for a total of $1.2 million. Still, this memoir should not suggest that the ACP never received a rejection letter. We received those letters from Z. Smith Reynolds, Mary Reynolds Babcock, Kellogg, Ford, and Steele-Reese Foundations—and these are just the major rejections I remember. One rejection came from Booth Ferris; when I sent a copy of the proposal to Willis Weatherford, president at Berea College at that time, and asked him

---

19. Years later, I met the head of the Exxon Foundation at a conference and mentioned the ACP had received a grant that we appreciated very much, and we also appreciated Dick Johnson's continuing to provide advice to us after the grant had ended. A day or so later I had a call from Dick asking what I had said to his director. When I told him, he said that the director had come to his office and complained about his spending time helping a project Exxon was no longer funding. Since he could not call us in the future, he said we needed to call him; he wanted to stay up to date with work of the ACA and perhaps fund us again in the future.

why the request would have been rejected, he pointed out that I had referenced Berea College as an example of one of the colleges served and that the bank where Booth Ferris was housed had managed the large endowment of Berea College until recently. That example is just one that illustrates how a request can be rejected for a reason that is unrelated to the quality of the application.

I learned that applications can be rejected because of one word, such as "conference." An applicant for a fellowship added the words "if any" to a request to study the impact a certain writer had on her time in history. The reviewers said, "If she doesn't know that there was an impact, we should not fund her to try to find one." If the applicant had left those two words off, she would have been funded.

The proposals submitted by the ACP that were funded during my years as director included those to the Pew Charitable Trust ($845,000) for fellowships for as long as a year for science faculty; Exxon Education Foundation ($92,000) for workshops to train faculty and staff on the use of computers; and the National Science Foundation (NSF) for a day-long meeting of faculty in the sciences to identify their needs for teaching at small private colleges. NSF encouraged the ACP, and later the ACA, to write proposals to support the science programs at member colleges because "most of the colleges were not competitive by themselves." Several years later, the second grant from Pew was $1.2 million; and the third grant from Mellon was $150,000. (John Stephenson had written the first two.) We received several small grants, such as one initiated by an Elderhostel participant whose company gave $5,000 to support a volunteer in the ACP. But when the new director of the Appalachian Center moved in, limits were placed on my efforts to raise money.

A Scholar Becomes an Administrator[20]

When a new director of the Appalachian Center took office in 1985, I should have expected him to want to change the ACP. I had worked in higher education long enough to know that it is common for a strong leader who replaces another strong leader to want his imprint, not that of the former leader, to mark the programs that are part of his domain. However, Dr. Hougland, as acting director, had been so supportive of the College Program and the Program was so successful in bringing money into UK that I was totally unprepared to have the new director tell me shortly after he arrived that he wanted me to end the ACP by 1990—five years after his arrival.

Fortunately, the program developed by Stephenson and supported by Hougland, both of whom were well liked across the campus, had developed fans at UK by the time the new director arrived—including President Otis Singletary. Thus, I quickly got over the shock of being told to phase out a program developed only five years before. After all, the program had already brought over a million dollars from major national foundations to UK. Why would the University agree to kill such a "golden goose"? Why would the University take pride in having a reputation in one state when it had a presence in five? Where would the University find another program that attracted such interest from federal agencies and multiple foundations? Could the University close its eyes to the recognition the institution could garner by serving disadvantaged students across the region, not just in Kentucky?

---

20. This title comes from a comment made by the vice president of Research and Graduate Studies during my third visit with him to complain about the obstacles the new director was placing on my efforts to raise money. "You'll have to give him time," said the vice president; "he's never been an administrator before."

At my next meeting with this new director, a man who was a scholar admired by multiple researchers of Appalachia, he indicated that he wanted me to focus on the public schools in eastern Kentucky. My response was that I had made commitments to numerous funders that I felt professionally and personally obligated to honor, and those commitments were not related to working with public K-12 schools. Hougland attended that meeting with the new director and me; afterwards, he wrote a note to me saying I would have to remember that my program was the **Appalachian** College Program, and he wrote to the new director that he would have to remember that my program was the Appalachian **College** Program. He also added to my note that he was concerned I would not want to work in the Appalachian Center under the new director, and he would help me find another job at UK if I wanted one.[21]

At our third meeting, the new director of the Appalachian Center pointed out his focus was providing service to Appalachia; I replied that the colleges in the ACP did provide service to the region. He insisted that they do not serve the region; they exploit the region—just like coal companies—by not paying taxes and not paying staff and faculty adequate salaries. Then he asked if I knew how many hungry people could be fed by one $30,000 fellowship. My response was that more could be fed if the Appalachian Center closed.

After this meeting, I went to see Stephenson and said, "You got me into this position, now tell me what I should do." He said that I could "quit." I said I did not want to quit; I liked the job of working with the college deans and faculty. He said I could "fight" the new direction

---

21. I didn't want a different job; I wanted a different boss.

the Center was taking under the new leadership. I said that I was tired of fighting; fighting takes too much time. He said, "You can shut up and do what you are told to do." I said, "Well, I guess I should do that." "Then," said Stephenson, "you won't be able to live with yourself." So, I continued resisting the efforts to end the ACP.[22]

The new director of the Center told me to stop raising money for the ACP; as a result, I worked with various faculty and chairs across the campus so they could submit proposals for funding new projects for the colleges in the ACP. At one point, a visitor to my office said, "No wonder your boss doesn't like you: your office is bigger than his, you have a bigger budget than he has, and you're raising more money than he is."

In later discussions, I told the new director that Dr. Hougland had told me that when the second Pew grant was funded, I would be eligible for a reclassification as a UK employee and, therefore, for a salary increase. The response was that he was not responsible for promises made by a previous administrator. When I asked if my secretary could be reclassified, his response was that he knew she deserved a promotion, but he could not recommend such a promotion because it would not be "political" for him to approve one. I suppose he meant that he could hardly argue that ACP staff needed to be promoted at the same time he was arguing that the ACP needed to be ended.

By the summer of 1985, I had developed good relationships with multiple foundations and a few federal agencies. My resolve to continue building the program supporting faculty at private colleges was

---

22. There's an Appalachian saying: "If everyone's troubles were hung on a line, you would choose yours and I would choose mine." For the several years I stayed in the Appalachian Center, I often thought that as miserable as my new boss made me, I probably made him even more miserable.

strengthened by the knowledge that people like Bill Bowen at Mellon, Helen Cunningham (later replaced by Ellen Burbank) at Pew, Bob Watson at NSF, Dick Johnson at Exxon, Tom Carroll at the Fund for the Improvement of Postsecondary Education (FIPSE), and multiple others connected to major financial resources believed in the work being accomplished by the ACP. Different sources of support came at various times from those at the local level: multiple department chairs and administrators at UK. David Roselle, who replaced Dr. Singletary as president at UK, was very supportive, offering funding from his discretionary account for ACP administrative costs. And Singletary himself helped after he retired and the ACP had become the ACA and moved to Berea.

At one point, when the ACP was submitting a proposal to NSF, the new director of the Appalachian Center told me I could not submit such a proposal because the ACP was going to be phasing out its programs. Paul Eakin, chair of the Math Department, submitted the request and named me the co-principal investigator of the project. At another time, Douglas Foard, a former James Still Fellow when he was a faculty member at Ferrum College, contacted me after he became a program officer at the National Endowment for the Humanities (NEH). He said that he had benefitted so much from the fellowship he received that he wanted to do something for the ACP now that he was in a position to do so. We discussed several ideas and decided the ACP would submit a request for funding to conduct a program where nationally recognized speakers could come to the region and make presentations around a central topic at multiple ACP colleges. When I told the Center director about the possibility, he explained that he was working on a proposal to NEH, and I could not be competing with his requests. After I cancelled the ACP plans for the NEH submission and the deadline for submissions had passed, the Center director told me he had cancelled his plans to submit a request to NEH and sent his proposal to the Rockefeller Foundation.

When Mellon funded the fellowships and travel grants for humanities faculty for a third time, one condition they placed on a future award was that the ACP would seek endowment funds to support these fellowships. I had said in that proposal that I would ask "someone **like** Willis Weatherford" to chair a board to lead the effort to raise the money; Tish said the Mellon board was pleased I would be working with Dr. Weatherford. I had not told Dr. Weatherford I had used his name; I had not expected Mellon to focus specifically on him as the person who would help. When I drove to NC to visit Weatherford a few days later and asked him to help, his response was that he would be happy to help, but that I should not establish a "board" because "board" implies the members would control me and I did not ever want anyone to think he or she controlled me. We established a "council" and invited Joe Smiddy, a retired college president from Tennessee; A.D. Albright, who had been a vice president at UK, president of the KY Council of Higher Education, and president of two Kentucky universities; Sam Hurst, a UK graduate and entrepreneur who had developed several businesses; and others in similar positions to help raise the endowment.

I sent letters to several possible funders for the endowment and got rejections from each. One was to Mary Bingham; she and her husband had sold the *Louisville Courier-Journal* and established a foundation. When my request was rejected, Mary Katherine Tri in the Development Office took the letter to Bill Sturgill, chair of the UK Board of Trustees; he took the letter to Mary Bingham and came back with a check for $500,000 to endow the fellowships for humanities faculty.[23] Mrs. Bingham said she "wanted to honor James Still with the fellowships,[24] help lots of colleges she couldn't help directly, and get UK off her back." In my letter of appreciation to her, I said her gift would do the first two, but I could make no promises about the third.

When Ellen Burbank, my program officer from Pew, learned that Mrs. Bingham had endowed the James Still Fellowships in the humanities, she wanted to know if I would ask her to endow the fellowships in the sciences. I told her I had promised Mrs. Bingham that I would not ask her for any other funding. Ellen said that she had not made that promise. I scheduled the next fellowship review session at a hotel in Louisville and invited Mrs. Bingham and Ellen to join us at dinner. I sat Ellen next to Mrs. Bingham. Later Ellen told me that when she said to Mrs. Bingham, "It must be wonderful to be able to fund so many wonderful projects like the Appalachian College Program," Mrs. Bingham said, "Yes, but it does limit where I can socialize and not have to worry about someone asking me for money; I like coming to Alice's events because I don't have to worry about anyone asking me for money." Ellen said that then she could not bring herself to ask Mrs. Bingham to endow the fellowships being funded by Pew.

---

23. Although Pew had funded year-long fellowships for science faculty, the Mellon grants for humanities faculty were still only for summer sessions. The endowment would produce about $25,000 each year—enough to fund six to eight fellowships.

24. Mrs. Bingham had written a review of Mr. Still's first book, *River of Earth*, in 1940; they had remained friends since then.

The Appalachian College Program (1980-1994)

Formation of the Deans' Council

My first year at the Appalachian Center, I learned that to promote the fellowship opportunities, the Center had sent information to the private colleges in the region, expecting the deans to disseminate it; but faculty from Emory & Henry and a couple of other colleges were the only ones applying. Faculty receiving fellowships were returning to their home campuses and promoting the opportunities to their colleagues, and the next year faculty from the same colleges were applying. It seemed as though the academic deans from the other colleges were just throwing the news about the awards into the trash.[25]

I started visiting the colleges and asking the deans to invite faculty to attend a meeting with me so I could describe the fellowship opportunities and then meet individually with faculty interested in submitting a proposal. One agenda in my calendar showed that I had met from 7 a.m. until 9:30 a.m. with faculty at Lee College; 11:30 a.m. until 1:30 p.m. at TN Wesleyan; from 4-5:30 p.m. at Maryville and from 7-8:30 p.m. at Carson-Newman, all in TN. The next day I met with faculty at Milligan and King, both in TN, and Emory & Henry in VA. Then I drove to West Virginia Wesleyan for an early meeting the next day. At the end of that year, I realized it would be easier for me to invite the academic deans to a meeting at UK than for me to visit thirty-seven (the number at that time) separate colleges every year. I could give the deans updates on funding and criteria for awards and make suggestions about information the fellowship applicants should include

---

25. I later came to realize that some academic deans did not want their faculty applying for fellowships—especially fellowships that required them to leave their campus for a year, leaving the deans to find replacement faculty for that year—no easy task in rural regions.

in their applications. Thus, the Deans' Council was formed, and my travel could focus on visits to foundations, with occasional visits to member colleges, especially ones not submitting many applications.[26]

The first fellowships were for humanities faculty; those for faculty in math and science followed soon afterwards. Eventually, funding was available for faculty in every field. When the Pew funding ended and the foundation decided to focus their funding on areas of need outside private colleges, Tish Emerson, a program officer at Mellon, convinced the Mellon trustees to fund faculty in the humanities and sciences. She argued that Mellon supported Colleges of Arts and Sciences, so the foundation should support faculty in both academic areas. McCune, Hearst, and other foundations provided the money that supported fellowships for faculty in the arts and professions.

Kentucky Elderhostel (Now Road Scholar)

When I left Eastern KY University, where I was working with the division of Conferences and Institutes, to a similar office at UK, I wanted the KY Elderhostel office that I had helped establish moved to my office at UK. The national Elderhostel office approved the move. By this time, the program involved about twenty colleges and state parks in KY, offering sixty or more weeks of programs each year. When I mentioned to the dean at EKU that I was moving to UK and wanted to move the Elderhostel program with me, he said he would see it go anywhere before he would see it go to UK. I said I could understand that so all I

---

26. Once, when I was talking about how impressed I was with the faculty at the ACP colleges, the person to whom I was talking said, "You only see the strong faculty; the weak ones hide when you're coming to campus because they know you're going to want them to do more than they are already doing."

would ask is that a board be established to oversee programs in KY and I would chair the board. When the dean talked to the president at EKU, the president said, "The only thing worse than losing the program to UK would be having it at EKU run by someone at UK; let her move it." When I left the office at UK where I was arranging meetings and events for outside groups to the Appalachian Center to administer the grant for the James Still Fellowships, I continued the work as state director for KY Elderhostel, and twenty percent of my salary was paid by the income from that program, reducing the amount that had to come out of the Mellon grant for salaries.

I hired Sister Eileen O'Connor to help manage the state Elderhostel program, and a recent college graduate to oversee Elderhostel programs hosted by UK. In just a few years, the UK Elderhostel program began to show some large expenditures, as well as some generous income. One day as I was leaving my office, a dean at UK called to tell me that the University was going to send auditors to my office the next day to look at records related to the Elderhostel programs. He said I should give them anything they requested. Since I was going to be on a plane the next day, when the auditors were scheduled to come, I called my assistant and told her to call Sister Eileen and tell her to wear her habit when the auditors came. They would not know they were coming to question a nun. The next day when I called the secretary to find out how the meeting went, I asked if Sister Eileen had worn her habit. She said she had not, but she did have her cross on; and when the auditors asked to see the Elderhostel assistant, she had said, "Oh, you mean Sister Eileen." When I asked Eileen what they wanted to know, she said they wanted to know what Elderhostel was; she told them and gave them catalogs to send to their parents, and they left.

It never occurred to me that if the director of the Appalachian Center wanted the ACP to end, he also wanted the state Elderhostel office to leave the University—until a contract from the National Elderhostel office in Boston arrived requesting UK's approval for the state office to be at UK for another year. When I took the contract to the Center director to be signed, he reminded me that if he did not want the ACP at UK, he did not want the KY Elderhostel office to be at UK, and he had no intentions of signing the contract to keep it there. Fortunately, Martha Layne Collins had recently become governor of KY, and she had been on the state Elderhostel Advisory Council. When I was told that UK would not sign the contract, I called Gov. Collins' office and asked that she send a letter to President Singletary at UK thanking him for UK's leadership of KY Elderhostel, a program that represented one of the best examples of institutional collaboration in the Commonwealth. The next day, the signed Elderhostel contract was on my desk when I arrived at the office.

Restrictive Institutional Policies

Much of the work I was doing at UK contradicted bureaucratic policies designed to prevent rewarding donors, tipping workers, raising money creatively (and legally), and generally just doing good things. Elderhostel programs involved tours to horse farms and museums where the guides or organizations themselves expected to be tipped. Since UK did not allow such tips, I arranged with the hotels where we housed the Hostelers to add a miscellaneous charge that would generate income that could be sent as a contribution to the facilities visited (such as museums) that did not charge an entrance fee or as tips for the grooms who escorted our groups through the horse farms. I should have learned from that experience that UK would not like my spending money for a "birthday party" for James Still.

When the ACP hosted a birthday celebration for James Still, he had asked for a new typewriter (not a computer, a typewriter). I called Mrs. Bingham and asked if I could use $700 of the interest on the endowment she had established to buy the typewriter. Several months after the birthday party, I had a call from the University's "inventory patrol." The patrol person reported that I had purchased a typewriter, but it was not included on the inventory of equipment in our office.

"Where is it?" he asked.

"The typewriter was a gift," I explained.

The inventory patrolman explained "gift" was not an expenditure that could be paid with state money.

"But the donor of the endowment, Mrs. Bingham, had told me I could use money from the endowment income for the gift to Mr. Still."

"Mrs. Bingham cannot change the use of the income after the endowment has been established without her legally changing the original intent of the endowment," said the person who called.

I responded, "I don't intend to tell Mr. Still to give us the typewriter back, but perhaps he can leave it to us in his will. Perhaps we can consider the typewriter 'on loan' until then."

"Too late for that," said the spokesperson from inventory. "You have already called it a gift."

"Well, I don't intend to pay for this $700 gift."

Then I was told to call the president's office and ask that the payment come from his discretionary fund. I did and it was.

Another expenditure that raised the alarm from the UK accountants was the dozen roses I sent to Mary Bingham after her gift of $500,000 to endow the Still fellowships. I had paid for the roses with money from the general operating budget for the ACP; the University provided about $30,000 each year for our operations. This money was clearly "state" money. Finally, the UK accountant told me to call the president's office to get reimbursed from his discretionary account—again. I was acquiring a reputation at all levels of the University.

The accounting office also questioned the expenditure I made for bottles of Paul Newman salad dressings. On a flight from New York to Lexington, I had seen in a magazine that Newman's company was having a competition to find new recipes using his products. I bought about a dozen bottles of Newman's salad dressing and took the products to the ACP office. I told the staff that each person was to take at least one product home and create a recipe using it; we would then have lunch at the office with the dishes created; the student workers would pick the winning recipe to send to the competition; the prize was $50,000 to the winner's favorite charity; and the ACP would be that charity if anyone on the staff had a winning submission. One staff member asked what would happen if the winner didn't give the $50,000 to the ACP. I suggested she might not be working at the ACP after that. Her response was, "Perhaps I could get a better job if I had $50,000 to give to some office." We never had to test that theory since our submission did not win.

The accountants were disturbed that I had bought multiple bottles of salad dressing from a local grocery store and charged the purchase to a UK account. When I explained that I had bought the product for a fundraising event and I had money designated "for fundraising," from foundations funding the ACP, they said I should send them the paragraphs from the award letter that said I could use a part of the funds to raise money. I did, and that was the last I heard about that expenditure—even though we did not win the $50,000 or even enough to cover the cost of the salad dressings.

Finally, Henry Clay Owen, treasurer of UK, asked me to come to his office. When I went, he explained how I could avoid words that alert the finance staff to the possibility that I was spending state money inappropriately. First, I had to learn that all money at UK is considered state money even if it comes from a grant or a self-supporting program (such as Elderhostel). Then, Owen gave me a list of words never to use in any UK financial document. "Don't," he said, "call anything 'a gift'; call it 'a supply' or even 'equipment.' Don't refer to a 'birthday party'; that's 'an official University function.' If you want to have something printed off campus, have whoever created the item put a copyright emblem on it; then only that person can indicate where it should be printed." Eventually I learned other strategies for accomplishing worthy goals.[27]

Except for the person who replaced John Stephenson as director of the Appalachian Center, I had generous support from faculty and staff across UK. One example was when Paul Eakin, chair of the Math Department, called after he had learned I didn't have a computer on my desk. "That's like the pilot of the plane not having equipment to

---

27. Several years later, when the Berea ACA office opened, I called Henry Clay Owen to get a reference for an auditing firm. Then I asked, "Is your life any easier since I left UK?" His response was, "It may be easier, but it's a lot less interesting."

steer the plane," he said. He added that there were computers in the Math Department that were being used as door stops and he was going to bring one to me.

"Don't," I said, "think you can bring me a computer and plug it in at my office; I have one outlet and it already has five things plugged into it."

"Send me the key to your office, and I'll come over this weekend and wire your office."

"Don't you think I just need to call maintenance to add an outlet?"

"You can call maintenance and wait six months for the outlet, or you can send me your key."

I sent the key, and when I arrived on Monday, I had a computer and an outlet for it. Then, of course, I had to confess that I did not have a clue about how to use the computer. A student instructor was sent to meet with me several times a week with the expectation that I would learn all I needed to use the computer within a few weeks. It took much longer than that.

Saving the ACP; Becoming the FSP (Faculty Scholars Program)

Although the new director of the Appalachian Center ceased to demand that I end the Appalachian College Program, he imposed several bureaucratic requirements that he expected me to honor. For example, he wanted his assistant to approve all ACP expenditures before they were sent to the Graduate School for payment. He had his assistant, who could see the parking lot from her desk, note every time one of my staff or I left the office before 5:00 p.m.. He frequently told me I didn't need to come to a meeting being held at the Appalachian Center building; of course, I always went anyway, and I always waited until the meeting had started before I entered the room, stumbling in and apologizing for being late. I knew that he would not throw me out of the meeting in front of multiple University staff and faculty. When he prepared my evaluations every year, he compared my work to that of one of his administrative assistants; clearly, he thought I was also supposed to assist him. I kept expecting him to find a reason to end the Appalachian College Program. As it turned out, the ACP was not ended, it was simply moved and given a new name—the Faculty Scholars Program (FSP). Less than a year later, it would become the Appalachian College Association (ACA).

The Fellowship Review Committee for the ACP at UK was composed of the chairs of major disciplines in the humanities and sciences and the dean of the Graduate School. When these committee members learned I had been forbidden to send requests to funding sources, people on that committee and other faculty across the campus submitted proposals requesting money for ACP initiatives. For example, Charles Elton, chair of the Higher Education Department, sent a proposal to the Fund for the Improvement of Postsecondary Education (FIPSE) related to helping ACP colleges assess the impact of their educational programs on developing values, and it was funded for $257,000. Paul Eakin from the Math Department sent a proposal to the Appalachian Regional Commission (ARC) to work with ACP colleges in the process of trying to incorporate technology into their teaching; it was funded. Later, Paul sent one to NSF related to the teaching of math; when that one was funded, it was a grant to the Math Department with Paul and me being co-principal investigators.

When I told one of the staff in the office that handled grants and contracts that I wasn't sure I could get a signature for a preliminary proposal for a federal grant from an official University representative, he allowed me to send the proposal without a signature, saying, "If the agency wants to fund this, then they'll ask for the signature. And no one at UK will turn down money in hand."

This assertion that UK never turned down money proved false when the UK lawyers insisted the University reject $1.25 million from Pew because a clause in the contract for the money indicated disputes related to the project would be resolved in the courts of Pennsylvania.

UK wanted the contract to indicate disputes would be settled in the courts of KY since UK had sovereign immunity in KY. I pointed out that UK had accepted $845,000 from Pew several years before. The lawyer reviewing the new contract said, "I wasn't here then." I checked with UNC-Chapel Hill since that university had also recently received a grant from Pew. Their position was that their sovereign immunity would follow them to PA. When I told that to the UK lawyer, his response was, "That's UNC's interpretation, not ours." Stephenson, as president at Berea College, agreed to accept the funding on behalf of the program at UK. When I called Ellen with the suggestion that Berea College accept the grant and let the FSP (later the ACA) administer it, her response was, "Just tell me where to send the check before our board wants to keep it."

When the $500,000 from the Bingham Fund arrived at the University, David Roselle, the new president of UK, called me at home on a Saturday morning to congratulate me. When the money appeared on the budget for the Appalachian Center, the Center director reminded me I was not supposed to be writing proposals for funding the ACP. I explained that Bill Sturgill, chair of the UK Board of Trustees, had raised that money. Then the new Center director explained that the ACP was a program and not an official office of UK, so an endowment could not be established for it. My response was that since we didn't need to use the money until the Mellon money ran out in about two more years, we could wait until then to determine how the endowment would be managed. He didn't respond to my comment, but a few days later, I had a call from Dick Parsons, one of the administrators in the Development Office, saying that my boss at the Appalachian Center had returned his signed copy of the endowment agreement; and he had changed the wording in the agreement and taken my name off the signature list.

The director of the Appalachian Center had added "and other activities of the Appalachian Center" to the words indicating that the money was for supporting faculty from private colleges in the region. I told Dick that Mrs. Bingham didn't even know there was an Appalachian Center. His response was, "If you have some verbal agreement with her...." I stopped him in mid-sentence and told him the agreement was in writing, to read the letter accompanying the check. The response from Dick was that he would send the new document to me with a cover letter requesting that I make certain that the wording was correct, change what was not correct, sign the final copy, and return it directly to him. Several months before this episode in the development of the ACP, a long-serving vice president at UK, Lewis Cochran, had told me that nothing changes at the University until there is a crisis. After the call from Development, I called Dr. Cochran and said, "I think we have that crisis."

It should not have surprised me that shortly after I returned the endowment agreement to the Development Office with the original wording replacing the revised version, I was taken to task by the

Center director for raising money when I had been told not to, that I had been insubordinate and that if I failed to follow his instructions again, he would fire me.

I went immediately to the office of the University lawyers and was introduced to Nancy Rae. She told me that I could be fired "on the spot" for insubordination. I referenced a recent news story about an assistant coach at UK who had sent money to a recruit and asked the lawyer, "At what point did the assistant coach have the right to refuse to send money to a recruit as the head coach had ordered?" I said that if I were insubordinate it was because I had been asked to do something that I considered unethical, immoral, or even illegal. There are two things she said that I distinctly remember: one was that my position at the University was solid because my recommendations came from representatives of foundations and federal agencies—people from off the campus—people whose views carried more weight than the opinions of those on the campus; the second was that if I were fired, she would take my side when we went to court.

Immediately after that meeting, Nancy contacted Wimberly Royster, the vice president of Research and Graduate Studies, to whom the director of the Appalachian Center answered, and recommended that he separate the ACP from the Appalachian Center before there was an episode that would create publicity about the University that "could damage everyone."[28] Royster called me and asked where I would like to be located. My response was, "Put me in the Education Department; my degree is from there. Put me in the Graduate School

---

28. I learned later that both the chair of the Math Department and the chair of the College of Education had already told Royster that he should move the Appalachian College Program out of the Appalachian Center.

if you think the ACP is essentially a graduate program. Put me in the extension division of the University if you think my program is for support of people not housed at UK. Just get me out of the Appalachian Center." We concluded the Graduate School was the best base for the ACP, in part because the dean of the Graduate School was already serving on the ACP review committee. The only objection the director of the Appalachian Center had to losing the ACP was that he did not want there to be two programs at UK with "Appalachian" in their titles. The name of the Appalachian College Program (ACP), once the program was housed in the graduate school, was changed to the Faculty Scholars Program (FSP).[29]

When the final document from the Bingham Foundation came, there was a sentence in it indicating that if the ACP should ever close or leave the University, UK could do whatever it wanted with the Bingham money. I called John Stephenson and indicated my concern: "This is a good reason for the University to get rid of the ACP." John assured me that my fear was unfounded, that once the document was in the UK file, no one would remember that sentence. Still, I contacted the lawyer for the Bingham Foundation to talk with him about the sentence. His response was, "We'll say that if the ACP ever leaves UK or closes, the endowment income can be used to bring students from Appalachia to UK."

That was a bad idea since ACP colleges wanted students from Appalachia to come to their campuses, and the money was given to strengthen those colleges, not to encourage students to come to UK. When the

---

29. Once when I introduced Dan Reedy, dean of the Graduate School, as the man "to whom I now answer," his response was, "Those of you who know Alice know she answers to no man."

lawyer asked how I wanted UK to use the money if the ACP was not using it, I suggested that the income be used to provide graduate fellowships at UK for students graduating from ACP colleges. At that time, there were few of the participating colleges offering graduate programs. So that is what the final agreement said. However, the first year after the ACA had opened in Berea and the fellowships were to be awarded, a flyer promoting these new awards said the money could be awarded to any student "from Appalachia." I called UK and pointed out that the language in the endowment agreement said the money was "for students graduating from private Appalachian colleges." I trust that phrase has been honored ever since—but I haven't seen any of the publicity recruiting applicants for years.

Involving the Graduate Deans of the Regional Research Universities

In the mid-1990s, our third grant from Mellon included our plans for continuing the fellowships after this latest round of funding. I had written that we would **try** to raise an endowment. Shortly after getting the grant and realizing I would need to raise the endowment, but not wanting to take the time to attend a workshop on fund-raising, I sent my assistant to one. She returned saying that if a foundation has funded your program, you should not expect their funding to continue; foundations like to build bridges to new programs, not sustain them. I was on the verge of taking that advice when the academic dean from Wheeling Jesuit College in WV, who happened to be at my office, said, "I still think you should go to New York and at least thank Mellon for the decade of funding; I babysat for Neil Rudenstine's children when I was at Harvard" (and Rudenstine was in graduate school there). Now Dr. Rudenstine was the executive vice president at Mellon.

The dean from Wheeling and I traveled to New York for a visit to The Mellon Foundation. After a few minutes of casual conversation, I mentioned the appreciation of the ACA colleges for the funding from Mellon as well as my understanding that Mellon's staff would not want us to come back to the foundation for additional funding. Rudenstine said the program officers did not want us to come back for the same program or purpose, but "what do you want to do next?" I said, "Give me sixty seconds and I'll think of something."

My response was I wanted funding for fellowships to faculty from ACP colleges to base their research at any of the major research universities in the five-state region served by the ACP—University of Kentucky, West Virginia University, University of North Carolina-Chapel Hill, University of Tennessee-Knoxville, Virginia Tech, and University of Virginia; fellows would not be limited to residency at UK. The graduate deans from those universities agreed to serve on the Review Committee for future awards (or to send their associate deans to review).[30]

The graduate deans surprised me with their strong support of the fellowship program. The only time I remember one not attending a review session was during a snowstorm; they spoke highly of the

---

30. The first time I met the graduate deans, I was struck by how dignified the dean from UVA looked. I thought he would be reluctant to devote time to fellowships for faculty at small private colleges. However, when the deans began talking about priorities for awards and one said the only standard is the quality of the application, it was Alexander Sedgwick, the graduate dean from UVA who said, "I don't agree; I think we need to consider how many opportunities the applicant has had to do research." When I saw Dr. Sedgwick's obituary recently, I was struck by all the comments about his interest in and support of minorities and women at UVA. The ACA was fortunate to have him and the other five graduate deans supporting faculty and students at ACA colleges.

ACA, and, while they pointed out that they could not get an ACA faculty member admitted to one of their graduate programs, they could "grease the wheels" of the admissions process. They agreed to waive out-of-state tuition for ACA faculty taking courses at their universities. The dean from UT, Bud Minkle, put ACA faculty into grant applications to NSF, and UT hosted the first ACA Summit at no cost. UT had a large conference center in downtown Knoxville where lodging and meals, as well as multiple meeting rooms, were available. A recently retired department chair at VA Tech led the ACA's first major grant ($1 million) for technology, providing multiple workshops for faculty from ACA colleges—at an average cost of about $250 per participant, including meals and lodging.

Since the ACA could not apply to the Jessie Ball duPont Fund (because the ACA was not one of the nonprofits the duPont family had identified for funding), VA Tech received a grant from Jessie Ball duPont to fund three years of training for ACA students to be technical assistants who could help faculty on their home campuses with instructional technologies. UNC-Chapel Hill wrote and received a grant from duPont to work with one ACA college in each of the five states of the service region to establish practices that would promote economic development. When ACA deans complained about the difficulty of finding temporary faculty to replace those away on a fellowship, the graduate deans suggested the ACA deans could consider their graduate students who had finished all but their dissertations (ABDs).[31] And the graduate deans looked for opportunities to attend

---

31. I never heard of an ACA dean who pursued the possibility of placing one of the ABD students in his or her classrooms to replace faculty away on a fellowship experience. Why? I can only imagine some of the deans were intimidated by the idea of having faculty who were nearing completion of graduate degrees at such prestigious research universities.

ACA Summits and speak with students who had received ACA grants about graduate schools and job opportunities.

Still, many ACA presidents did not "take kindly" to the rejection of any of their faculty's requests for fellowships. During the early years of online degrees, the graduate deans rejected every application from faculty members wanting to get such a degree. Many of the college presidents really wanted their business faculty to get doctoral degrees, and they did not care if the degrees were online. Frequently, I would be asked by ACA presidents why these graduate deans were making decisions they (the presidents or academic deans) should be making. I could never convince some of them that having the fellowship recipients chosen by a panel that consisted of academic deans from ACA colleges and graduate deans from major research universities gave the ACA the kind of credibility that helped assure future funding.

Fortunately, Tish Emerson at Mellon told me to be sure and make it clear in documents I left when I retired that the graduate deans had to be (or be represented) on the Fellowship Review Committees or the endowment for those awards that Mellon had provided would be jeopardized. Since the endowment was funded by multiple foundations, federal agencies, and individuals, funding from all those agencies and people could be jeopardized if the endowment agreement was not honored. As a Johns Hopkins University Press book on *How to Run a College* explains: An endowment is "given by donors over the years to provide perpetual support for faculty, students, programs, and so on. These restricted funds must be spent according to the donor's wishes, and the trustees of the institution function as fiduciaries in their investment and expenditure."[32] I understood that graduate deans at major universities come and go, but I assumed that the current deans would encourage the participation of their replacements; perhaps, associate graduate deans would continue to evaluate the proposals. The intent of involving those graduate deans was to assure donors to the fellowships and grant programs that the integrity of the awards would be secured by always including outside evaluators, that the ACA would not accept evaluations that came only from those internal to the ACA or to the member colleges.[33]

Program Evaluation

In 1989, I was informed that every program at UK had to be evaluated by an outside evaluator every ten years. In seeking an outside evaluator, I called John Chandler, retired president of Williams College and then president of the Association of American Colleges and Universities (AAC&U), expecting he would give me the names of several possible evaluators. Instead, he said he would do the evaluation. He had spent his first two years of college at one of the ACP colleges, and he felt that the AAC&U had not done enough to address the needs of small private colleges.

---

32. Brian C. Mitchell and W. Joseph King, *How to Run a College:* Johns Hopkins University Press, (Baltimore: Johns Hopkins University Press, 2018), 25.

33. I learned later that for NEH and other federal funding agencies, if money awarded for an endowment by that agency is misused, NEH will not stop the misuse; the agency will just tag the association as one not to be considered for future funding. A less formal policy for some of the other ACA funders was that the current officers could choose whether to request a return of the money awarded. Again, however, such misuse would negatively impact the possibility of future funding.

After Chandler had completed the evaluation of the Appalachian College Program, I held a meeting in Washington, D.C., at the Phi Beta Kappa office. Douglas Foard, the former Ferrum College faculty member, James Still Fellow, and NEH program officer mentioned earlier, was now executive secretary of Phi Beta Kappa. Those invited to attend the Washington meeting included individuals from each of the funders of the Appalachian College Program, two representatives from the graduate deans' review committee, representatives from the ACP Deans Council, the president of the ACA board, and Willis Weatherford (former Berea College president). Jon Fuller, who had been director of the Great Lakes Colleges Association (GLCA) for fifteen years, chaired the meeting. There was a surprising number of representatives from the foundations and federal agencies that had funded the ACP at UK, including NSF, ARC, Exxon, Mellon, and Pew.

Minutes or a transcription of this meeting should be in the ACA archives. Although I wrote those minutes, I remember few pertinent comments from them: Jon Fuller had been working with a group of colleges in the Washington area, but that organization had disbanded. His most memorable comment was the ACP should never try to raise an endowment because there could come a time when the ACP was no longer needed. When there was criticism that the ACP might be involved in too many projects, Bud Minkle (graduate dean from UT) pointed out that having multiple projects was important to keep a program and its staff from becoming stale.

Shortly after the Washington meeting, we held a meeting at UK for all the deans of the member colleges—the Deans' Council. When John Chandler mentioned involving the presidents in the governance of the program, there was an outcry among the deans: "The presidents will destroy this program!" Weatherford said that he was surprised by the lack of respect for presidents in the room. But, once the deans were relegated to a position behind the presidents in making decisions for the work of the ACP (later the ACA), it became increasingly difficult for the focus to remain on faculty and students. Program officers from the major foundations and federal agencies funding the ACA were able to attend many of the ACA board meetings and other special events, and they were invaluable in keeping the focus of the program on faculty and students. But presidents are charged with addressing financial needs across their campuses: (1) annual giving and deferred contributions, (2) enrollment, (3) retention, (4) capital construction, and (5) endowments. Academic excellence is not usually at the top of concerns for presidents at colleges facing the possibility of closure. Yet, when alumni contribute to their alma maters, they usually do so because of faculty who were major inspirations to them; few alumni remember who the president of their college was when they were students.

Efforts by UK to Keep the FSP

David Roselle became president of UK in July of 1987 and almost immediately became an avid supporter of the ACP. His support came, at least in part, because he started work at UK on a day when the only official event on the campus was a gathering of ACP fellowship recipients with William Lipscomb, a Nobel Prize-winning chemist from Harvard, the keynote speaker who spoke about the relationship between the sciences and the humanities. Staff from the public relations office at UK used the event to highlight Roselle's new appointment. A year or so later, Roselle and the governor of KY were battling over how to respond to an accusation by the NCAA about the basketball program at the University.[34] So, when Roselle cancelled a scheduled lunch meeting with a group of presidents from ACP colleges to meet with the governor and asked if he could meet with the ACP presidents at breakfast, I was pleased he didn't just cancel and not reschedule.

Some of the presidents who were working to develop the Appalachian College Association as an independent nonprofit association had come to meet with President Roselle, several UK vice-presidents, and me to discuss separating the Faculty Scholars Program (previously the Appalachian College Program) from the University rather than trying to develop the ACA as an independent association and continue the FSP at UK. As a result of the change in Roselle's schedule, when he met with the college presidents and me, there were no other UK administrators in attendance. When Roselle understood we were trying to move the FSP to make it independent of the University, his response was, "But this is **our** program."

I replied that there were people on the campus who didn't think the University received enough benefit from the program for the money (about $30,000 plus overhead) UK contributed—that the grant money went to small private colleges and UK didn't even get to keep the interest earned. Roselle's response was (and I remember this vividly), "I am sorry to hear there are people on this campus who think

---

34. When money was found in an envelope to a recruit for UK's basketball program, and the NCAA investigated, Roselle hired a judge for a full investigation when many people wanted him to stonewall the investigation. Even though his decision and the resulting "house-cleaning" led to years of success by the basketball team, with the governor's opposition to Roselle's decision, Roselle believed that his staying at UK would hurt instead of help the University. After only two years, he left UK and became the president of another major university in another state (Jerry Tipton, *Lexington Herald-Leader*, April 14, 2012).

like that; it isn't important what UK is getting from the program; what's important is how the program is benefiting higher education in the region. If our work improves the colleges, we'll eventually get better graduate students." When I mentioned that as an independent association, the colleges would pay membership dues to help fund the operations of the office, Roselle asked how much more money I needed for administration of the office. I don't remember the amount I gave him, but his answer was that the money could come from the president's discretionary fund.

At lunch with the vice presidents, one said, "I told Roselle not to let Alice give away the farm." I replied, "But John Stephenson told me when I was hired that the purpose of a Land Grant University is to give itself away." Shortly after that meeting, Roselle left the University. Then I was told that anything Roselle had promised did not have to be honored by the new UK president. And it wasn't.

Leaving the University

Charles Wethington, the president who replaced Roselle, had served as chancellor for the Community College System when that system was part of UK. His experiences with the state-wide system gave him a perspective that perhaps some of the previous presidents did not have; once he became president of UK, plans for the FSP (formerly ACP) changed. In discussions with Ellen Burbank from Pew and Tish Emerson and Liz Duffy from Mellon, President Wethington made it clear that from his perspective, a program involving thirty-seven colleges with only about twenty percent of them being located in KY was not a program that UK should be supporting.

UK seemed uninterested in encouraging major foundations to look favorably upon the University. After the meeting with Wethington, I took Tish and Liz to lunch at the UK Faculty Club. When we were leaving, Liz realized her coat was not in the cloakroom. We were convinced that someone had taken her coat by mistake and would return it when she found the receipt in the pocket of the coat. But I called the president's office, assuming some effort by the public relations office would be made to find Liz's coat or replace it. No one from UK ever contacted her about the coat, not even a secretary. When I sent her a gift certificate from Bloomingdale's, which is just around the corner from the Mellon offices in New York, so she could replace the coat, Liz called to tell me she could not accept a gift from a beneficiary of Mellon's largesse, but she did think that someone should tell UK that "it is not wise to send a representative of a major foundation home without her coat."

A major administrator at UK told me that if I left UK, the graduate deans from the other universities would not be willing to serve on the Fellowship Review Committee. I called each one and heard similar stories from each: the WVU graduate dean said that it would be easier for him to serve on a committee of the ACA than it was for him to serve on a committee for a UK program. Folks at WVU questioned why he was helping one of their major competitors. The UNC-Chapel Hill associate dean for graduate studies responded by saying, "Of course, we'll stay on the committee; just know we're here to cooperate with you in any little scheme you want to hatch." My reputation had now spread across the region.

A total of $4,494,363 awarded to the ACP between 1979-1990 included the following: two grants for $280,000 each and one for

$150,000 for fellowships and $25,000 for planning from Mellon (for a total of $735,000); two grants for $845,000 and $1,200,000 (for a total of $2,045,000) for fellowships from Pew; $92,000 and $10,000 for computer training from Exxon (a total of $102,000); $500,000 from Bingham Foundation to endow humanities fellowships (i.e., James Still Fellowships) at UK; $257,000 from the US Department of Education for assessment; $10,000 from the KY Dept. of Education for the UK Theatre Department to conduct workshops on producing dramatic productions with limited budgets; $24,000 from TVA for workshops on computer networking; $90,000 from ARC for development of computer networks; $24,915 for a conference to identify needs of science programs; $107,817 for training related to networking plus $113,000 for internet connections and $73,495 for Calculus Reform from NSF (totaling $319,227); $55,000 plus $357,136 worth of computer labs from AT&T (totaling $412,136).[35] The roughly $4.5 million was a significant amount of support for the ten years of the program at UK; but in the fifteen years the Appalachian College Association was an independent non-profit, contributions from foundations, federal agencies, and individuals totaled almost $50 million. When I retired, I believed the ACA was set to continue raising $3-5 million each year—or more—to expand support for the faculty and students at member colleges.[36]

---

35. These figures were compiled from notes in my files, not from official reports from UK. I cannot vouch for their accuracy, but I am confident they are close to, if not the same as, reports at UK.

36. Note again, the primary focus of the program and the association was always on faculty and students.

Chapter 4

The Appalachian College Association (1990-2008)

Background

After the evaluation by John Chandler, I continued to administer the Faculty Scholars Program, working with Dan Reedy, dean of the Graduate School. In 1989 (or thereabouts), a group of presidents from the colleges participating in the Faculty Scholars Program met—including John Stephenson (Berea), Tom Courtice (WVW), Fred Bentley (Mars Hill), Doug Orr (Warren Wilson), and Tom Morris (Emory & Henry). Their goal was to create the Appalachian College Association (ACA), inviting a select group of the presidents of colleges in the five-state region of central Appalachia to join and pay a fee to help support the Association. When I learned that the plan was to limit membership to financially strong colleges in the region, I contacted Stephenson and told him that the purpose of the ACP had been (and I assumed the purpose of the new ACA was) to strengthen faculty of the institutions in central Appalachia and there were lots of strong faculty at weak colleges in the region. The committee developing the new consortium agreed, and Alf Canon, president of Warren Wilson from 1988-1991, became the director of the ACA on a half-time basis while he was also director of Church Relations for Warren Wilson.

After about two years, Canon became seriously ill and resigned his position with the ACA. By then it was obvious that having the ACP with the new name—FSP—at UK and the ACA somewhere else was not a model likely to promise much success.

All the new ACA office did during the few years it was based at Warren Wilson is not clear to me, but Dr. Canon did an excellent job of establishing the office and getting 501(c)(3) tax exempt status for it. One grant was funded by Teagle and Jessie Ball duPont (through ACA colleges on the list of colleges that could apply to duPont) to support a consultant who could travel the region and work with all the member colleges on deferred giving. Also, the office received a grant of $1.8 million from Mellon to provide funding for research projects of faculty and students. After Dr. Canon's death, money that had been collected for dues for ACA membership during the years he led the Association was designated for small ACA projects that were not funded by other resources. For example, a competitive program in visual arts for faculty and students across the ACA and workshops on techniques in painting and other media were funded by the Canon Fund.

The fact that ACA was formed by a group of college presidents helps explain the emphasis on helping each college with fundraising. But the focus of the Association was clearly faculty development, as was true for the Appalachian College Program. Almost twenty years after the launch of the ACA, when member presidents were asked what they wanted from the Association, the answer was, "We do not want the ACA to be a social organization for deans and presidents; we get that from the CIC and other places. We do not want the ACA to be a joint purchasing agency; we go through our state Councils for Independent Colleges for that. What we want from the ACA is faculty development" (Keener, p. 67). But I never found a way to keep the voice of the faculty at the forefront of ACA planning. While the academic deans were, I claimed, the voice of the faculty, most were more loyal to their presidents than to the faculty. The presidents were more likely to fire them than the faculty were.

When I was officially offered the position as the director of the ACA, I went to Vice President for Research and Graduate Studies Lee Magid to resign from my position at UK. She said that I didn't have to leave UK; there were other positions at UK that I could move to. My response was, "But the ACA is offering me a twenty-five percent raise." Despite the many years I had argued that my salary at UK should be higher than it was, the response had always been that there were no other UK staff positions similar to mine where a comparable salary could be used to establish my salary. The response from Magid this time was, "I think we could match that twenty-five percent." I left her office and accepted the ACA offer.[37]

Knowing that the new UK president, Dr. Wethington, had no interest in keeping a program focused on supporting private colleges across five states, my next step was to approach Dan Reedy, dean of the Graduate School and Lee Magid, vice president for Research and Graduate Studies, to plan the move of the program from the University. The conversation started amiably, with Reedy saying he was pleased to know that the "kids" had grown up and were prepared to leave the University and stand on their own. However, when I said,

---

37. Although there was a national search for a new director of the ACA, when Fred Bentley of the search committee came to UK to talk to me about becoming that director, I remember his saying, "I don't know why we are going through the motions and incurring the expenses of a national search when we clearly have a good candidate already in place." But there was a national search, and as much as I would have liked to see what I heard was a long list of applicants, I was never privy to that information.

"Let's talk about how to move the money in the UK accounts that was raised for the FSP," I could hear doors slamming all across campus. At that point there was over $2 million in the FSP account, and I didn't want to have the model the ACA presidents had rejected, with the ACA at one location and the FSP at another providing basically the same services.

Dan said, "We don't move money."

"But," I replied, "you just said you were happy to see the kids leave home."

"I'm happy to see the kids grow up and leave home, but I'm not giving them their inheritance until I die."[38]

"Dan, it is costing $150,000 to operate the UK office and it is going to cost $150,000 to operate the new office independent of UK; you don't want to waste your children's inheritance. Besides, maybe it's time for you to die."

One highlight of my professional career came in the weeks following that meeting with the graduate dean and vice president. I had notified my program officers at Pew, Mellon, Burroughs Wellcome, etc., about the possibility that the FSP would become the ACA, an independent not-for-profit association. When I called Bert Ifill, my program officer at Mellon at that time, to tell him that the leaders at UK had made it clear to me that money in the Mellon account was not mine to move, I distinctly remember Bert's response: "It may not be yours, but it is

---

38. A representative sent from the Exxon Foundation was waiting in my office to meet with me about a project when I returned from that meeting, and when I told him what had happened, he said, "Then you should have leaned across the table and said, 'And I'm here to help you go.'" This lawyer from Exxon is another person who has continued as a friend I still hear from occasionally.

ours, and if you want it moved, we'll move it." When Reedy called Ellen Burbank at Pew and told her he wanted to come to meet with her and assure her UK could continue to administer the Pew funds for science faculty even after I left to lead the ACA, I heard that her response was, "Don't come unless you bring Alice." They agreed on a date to meet, but by the time Reedy contacted me about that meeting, I had scheduled an annual meeting with Elderhostel directors from colleges across KY for the same day. When I told Reedy that I would not be able to go, he contacted Ellen to tell her he would come but I had a conflict in scheduling. Ellen's response was that if I could not come to Philadelphia, she would come to KY and we could meet whenever I had time during or after the Elderhostel meeting.

When several presidents on the ACA Executive Committee of the Board came to visit Reedy and Magid, an agreement was reached to leave all funding related to the FSP in place at UK but develop a subcontract to transfer administration of those funds to the ACA Berea office.

Shortly after I moved to the new office, I had a call from my program officer at Burroughs Wellcome.[39] It was about time for a new check to be sent for support of the fellowships Burroughs Wellcome was funding, and someone from UK had called to advise her that I had my hands full getting the new office opened, and the UK representative thought she should know that the University was better prepared to administer the Burroughs Wellcome grant than I was at the time. The Burroughs Wellcome representative had called me to ask if I felt overwhelmed by the move and wanted UK to handle their funding.

---

39. Her first name was Martha; I don't remember the last name. I think she left Burroughs Wellcome to go to medical school.

My response was, "There is no one at UK better prepared to administer the money than I am since I have been administering it for years."

Shortly after that conversation I had a call from someone in the development office at UK saying that I was being very unprofessional—I was soliciting funders for the ACA who had supported the FSP at UK. My response was that I was only staying in touch with those who had supported the ACP and FSP at UK now that we were moving the activities of those programs to the ACA in Berea. I was only asking funders to continue supporting what they had been supporting.

While there were many advantages to being in a small office with no bureaucracy, I knew that leaving UK meant leaving the many faculty at UK who either wrote proposals for grants serving the Appalachian colleges or helped me write them or served on the Fellowship Review Committees. Also, there were many resources on the campus that served my programs at UK well, from the accounting officers who maintained financial records to the marketing staff who designed and printed brochures for events and services. The College of Engineering submitted a proposal to NSF to operate a repair van that could travel across the ACA region and fix equipment related to science programs (but not computer equipment). The program remained at UK when the ACA was established at Berea, but once the second grant ended, NSF would not renew funding. UK was not willing to continue the service without outside funding, and there were not enough ACA college presidents who valued the service enough to pay to continue it. But many of the science faculty from the member colleges were disappointed to see the service end.

Once I was located at the ACA office in Berea, KY, it was unrealistic for me to expect faculty at ACA member colleges to help with ACA applications to funding agencies; most were teaching four to five courses each semester, advising at least one student organization, serving on multiple college committees, and helping with accreditation matters and strategic planning.

An illustration of how many of the presidents at ACA colleges viewed the ACA occurred when Danielle Carr-Ramdath from Mellon was visiting in the region. At a stop at one of the member colleges, Danielle suggested faculty from ACA colleges should rotate to provide an ACA staff person for a year. The president at that college responded to her by saying, "If you take one of my good faculty members for a year, I'll take my college out of the ACA." Late in my tenure at the ACA, Melissa Taverner, faculty member from Emory & Henry, did become a traveling scholar for the ACA on leave from her college for a year. She helped solicit students for NSF awards and assisted faculty at multiple ACA colleges submit proposals for grants related to the sciences. In many cases, the presidents of the member colleges were willing to support the ACA by paying dues to access opportunities for their faculty, but few were willing to make any other kind of contribution; and few were willing to share any of the good resources of their institutions. The financially weak colleges could not afford to share any of their resources, and most of the financially strong ones were afraid helping a weak college would "drag their college down." The presidents did add a small amount to their annual payment to address an immediate need or help develop the endowment. But it was always clear that the increase or contribution was an exception to the annual financial obligation.

I grew accustomed to having faculty tell me how blessed they had been by ACA benefits and how faculty at wealthier colleges envied them for the opportunities available through the ACA. One new dean at a college eligible to be an ACA member was surprised to learn that the president there did not want the stigma of being part of an organization with "Appalachian" in its name. He had been employed at a college that did belong to the ACA, and he knew the importance of the ACA for faculty development at a small college. He agreed to accept the new position only if he had access to the resources of the ACA. He said he would not leave the college where he was unless the president at the new college agreed to pay dues for ACA membership. And the president agreed—then added, "But the college can't afford to pay the dues for the coming year; we'll have to wait a year." The college librarian who learned of the president's position said, "I'll pay the dues for the coming year from my budget." From communications with other ACA librarians, he had learned how valuable the Central Library was to colleges like his. Alone, he could never replicate the resources provided by the ACA.

Sunsetting FSP Initiatives

A number of projects in the FSP needed to end or change so that continuing projects could be merged into the ACA. The Fund for the Improvement of Secondary Education (FIPSE) at the US Department of Education had funded an evaluation of graduates of the ACP colleges to determine if the goal of developing critical thinking and strong values was being realized. Willis Weatherford (retired Berea College president at the time) was on the committee that helped with the project, and I remember his saying that what we were trying to measure probably could not be measured but if the ACP didn't try, it was unlikely anyone else would. Tom Carroll from

FIPSE spoke at one of the meetings of ACP deans, and he pointed out that the grant to UK would have to conclude before the ACA could apply for new funding from FIPSE. As the grant to assess outcomes of the member colleges was continuing at UK, Karen Carey, the project director, organized the Appalachian College Assessment Consortium (ACAC) to provide funding for several years to determine the effectiveness of the college experience at ACA colleges. But, as usual, the colleges were not interested in continuing it once there were no funds available to cover the costs of operating the program.

NSF had funded a one-day workshop to identify the greatest needs of the science faculty at ACA colleges, inviting faculty in the sciences to UK to identify how NSF could help the colleges' science programs. One major need was storing and disposing of hazardous chemicals. A plan was developed to centralize a service that could pick up and dispose of such materials across the campuses, but there was so much variation in need and no company was interested in bidding to provide the service since it would have to cross state lines, so no proposal addressing the concern was ever fully developed.

Working with colleges across five states complicated the creation of contracts governing services because different states often had different policies and laws related to interstate services, such as power and other utilities. When UK offered to provide centralized purchasing for FSP colleges, few of the colleges had central purchasing offices; with each department buying its own supplies, it became complicated to determine if using contracts controlled by UK would save money. Carolina Biological offered to give ACA colleges a discount on purchases from their company, but only if all the colleges would buy from them. There were three or four colleges that insisted they had developed relationships with other vendors that their science faculty did not want to leave, but Carolina Biological finally agreed to give a discount to the other ACA colleges.

At the time of the move to Berea, the ACA was involved in a major dispute related to a software program designed by one of the Pew fellows. Exxon sent a lawyer from a firm in Dallas to help resolve the question: Rick Kneipper from Jones Day—an international law firm. The question was who was entitled to claim ownership or at least some part of the ownership: UK or the ACA or the home campus of the fellow or the fellow himself? After several years of discussions, it became obvious that by the time the issue could be resolved, the software would be obsolete, and the discussions were dropped. The ACA presidents did, however, develop a contract indicating that in the future, intellectual property rights related to the development of a marketable property would be divided among the fellowship recipient, the fellow's college, and the ACA, hopefully eliminating any discussions in the future about the right of any institutional site where the fellow might be stationed while developing the property. Kneipper continued to work with the ACA, serving on the Advisory Council and offering legal advice when appropriate.

A project based at the ACA when it was housed at Warren Wilson involved a series of roundtables to help the colleges learn more about strategies related to planned giving. With funding from Teagle and Jessie Ball duPont, a consultant was hired to work with ACA colleges that either had at least one planned-giving officer or agreed to hire one. The consultant would spend three days each year at each of the participating colleges. After three years, when grants for the project ended, the project ended.[40] While having extra help with fundraising would have been welcomed if there were assurances that having help would increase contributions, there were no such assurances. This was the typical response: if outside funding ended, the project ended. Fees for participation in the Central Library were paid because the immediate financial benefits outweighed those fees.

I often said that the presidents would approve any project if they did not have to pay to participate (beyond regular ACA dues), and they would reject any project for which participation required an added cost. One person asked if the presidents thought a project lost value if there was not funding beyond that of their institution. The simple fact was, I believe, that only two or three of the ACA colleges could afford to pay to participate in a project that would simply add value to their educational program when their finance offices were finding it difficult to pay for basic operating costs.

The Appalachian Regional Commission (ARC) gave $60,000 for the ACA based at Warren Wilson to send students to Washington for experiences working with federal agencies, but the grant ended when the ARC realized that some of the money was being used for travel expenses for the students when that was not a documented expense in the proposal; the full amount of the grant was to be used for administrative costs, not participant expenses. And the colleges would not cover the costs of travel, housing and meals for the participants.

During the move from UK to Berea, there were multiple special issues that had to be addressed. For example, everyone thought the

---

40. The proposal for this planned giving project and the final report submitted to the funders may be stored at Warren Wilson since that was where the project originated and concluded.

ACA office that had operated in NC had been incorporated there; it had not. When I developed Articles of Incorporation for the new office (by basically copying such articles from those of a similar organization), I took them to Frankfort, KY, to be recorded. The woman who reviewed that document said that I had given a post office box number for our address and the Articles needed the street address. She said I would have to take the form back to the lawyer who had developed them and get the change made. When I said, "But I developed them; we didn't have a lawyer," she replied, "Great, here is some whiteout and a typewriter; make the change and give the form back to me."[41]

There were questions about the nonprofit status of the ACA. When we learned the ACA had not paid some tax assessed on non-profit organizations, we appealed to the IRS, explaining our ignorance of the law and mentioning that the $30,000 penalty for our negligence would mean at least one less fellowship available for some deserving faculty member working for low pay in a disadvantaged region of the country. The IRS penalty was rescinded.

Utilizing Task Forces

When the ACA office was at Warren Wilson, the presidents established task forces to help identify projects they considered important. The office at Warren Wilson developed a project focused on planned giving and created a task force to expand it. Then

---

[41]. Here was a woman who thought like me: The fewer hoops to jump through (i.e., the fewer procedural requirements) the better. I was amazed by the fact that most requests for funding from a federal agency required fifty or more pages while many foundations required about five.

a survey was sent to all the presidents to identify other priorities: institutional assessment, faculty development, maintenance of scientific equipment, fine arts/visiting scholars, regional library networks, and high school-college partnerships.

NSF rejected a request for funding a project related to ACA college faculty working with local public schools to strengthen science and math teaching, saying there was no common theme or approach to the work proposed; with no central strategy there was no reason for the ACA to do what it proposed: provide centralized coordination. Later, the majority of the ACA presidents rejected a proposal that the association might develop to make working with local public schools a priority. Most of the colleges already had strategies for working with local schools and there was no reason to insist on a standard program for all colleges or even for a small subset of ACA colleges. Having most of the thirty-five or so colleges participate in a project usually made it easy to justify the time and expense of developing it. Having half a dozen or so of the ACA colleges wanting a coordinated approach to working with their local schools would not have made it cost-effective for the ACA to plan such an approach and raise money for it. While the ACA policy was that not all members had to participate in all projects, if a majority of the presidents had no interest in a proposed project, the project was seldom developed. What was encouraged was collaboration between or among the colleges that had developed a successful school-college program. The ACA never tried to see if any of the colleges did work with each other to explore the possibility of collaborating in this way, but if there was such development, none of the college deans told the ACA about it.

The task forces continued during the first year or so of operations at

Berea, but it was difficult for the presidents to find times to meet, even by conference call, and trying to address the needs of the individual colleges with one proposal involved a lot of compromise. It did not take long for the task forces to dissolve, and the Executive Committee for the Governing Board[42] assumed responsibility for identifying target areas for funding. Of course, meetings with funding agencies often ended with the program officers moving the ACA proposal in a direction that served the goals of the funders as well as those of the Association, leaving some ACA presidents frustrated that their specific ideas were not funded according to their specifications. It is worth remembering that when John Stephenson visited Mellon back in 1979 to ask for funding to support the Appalachian Center at UK, and Mellon said, "We don't fund centers," John did not walk away. The funding he negotiated for faculty at Appalachian private colleges led to the creation of the ACA and the many benefits it provides.

Location and Staff in Berea

Stephenson arranged for the ACA to have a three-room, second floor apartment where the Mountain Association for Community Economic Development (MACED) was located on the ground floor; the ACA could use some of MACED's resources, such as a large copier and a large conference room. To my surprise, my assistant at UK,

---

42. All presidents of the member colleges served as the ACA Governing Board; initially, the Executive Committee of the Board was a representative from each state and a chair, vice-chair, secretary-treasurer—all chosen by the whole Board for two-year terms. By 2003, an academic dean and a member of the Advisory Council were also added. Virginia and North Carolina shared a representative. In 2006, the Board voted to eliminate the position of vice-president; the vice-president seldom had any significant responsibilities, and the Board decided that having the person who had served as treasurer move into the presidency would be wise. A president was added to the Executive Committee as an at-large member.

Eugene Zita, wanted to move to Berea to continue working with me. Initially, she had the living room of the ACA apartment as her office, and I had what had been the bedroom. Mellon sent a large Ficus plant to celebrate our move, and we housed it in the kitchen. We had to struggle to keep the plant alive, but we were determined to do so; the plant became a symbol of our relationship with Mellon, and we wanted it to thrive. After a couple of years of struggling to keep the plant alive, we took the advice of a local horticulturalist and put it on the front porch of the offices one summer; shortly thereafter someone stole it. Eugene asked if I wanted her to report the theft to the local police. "No," I said, "this way I can imagine that the plant is being well nurtured and our relationship with Mellon is strong—without having to worry about trimming, watering, feeding, and shading the plant."

After about a year in Berea, we hired John Hennen to promote the fellowships and other opportunities available to faculty; the kitchen became his office (though he was visiting the colleges most of the time and was seldom in the office). John had recently graduated with his Ph.D. from WVU and had published a book based on his dissertation, *The Americanization of West Virginia*. When Eugene asked how, out of all the applications we received, I had chosen John, I replied that one of his references was someone I knew whose judgment and honesty I trusted without reservation. John was great as an ACA representative promoting the fellowships, travel grants and other opportunities provided for faculty at member colleges. As a recent Ph.D. student, he could easily relate to young faculty across the five-state central Appalachian region. As a single person, he had no reservations about traveling most of every month to visit the colleges and promote the ACA benefits. And he was comfortable living out of his pickup truck, so his travel expenses were minimal.

I remember three John Hennen stories during the year he worked with the ACA: (1) When he came to be interviewed, we sat in the kitchen of the apartment as I explained how I hoped we could work together as colleagues and did not want people thinking of me as his boss. His response was, "You know, people will think of me as your boss since I'm the guy." My response was, "That's okay so long as I'm making twice what you make." (2) At the first annual meeting of the presidents after John was hired, I was telling one of the presidents Hennen's comment about people thinking he was the boss since he was the male in the office. That president's response was, "Don't be silly; we're way past the time when people thought like that." Then that president's wife came over to us and asked if she was interrupting. I said, "No, we were just discussing John Hennen; have you met John?" Her reply was, "Oh, is he your new boss?" (3) After his first visit across the region, meeting with faculty at the member colleges, John had a great idea. He thought that we should "unionize the faculty." My response was, "That's a great idea, but not on my watch." I was very sure that the last thing most of the presidents on the ACA board wanted was for the faculty to unionize.

Although Hennen had agreed to stay with the ACA for at least three years (the length of the most recent grant for fellowships), he left after about a year to take a tenure-track job at Morehead State University in KY. He called me several years later to ask if there were any vacancies at the ACA he could apply for; I said, "Not at this time." He stayed at Morehead until he retired from full-time teaching. I had multiple employees who served as the liaison between faculty at the member colleges and our office, but none were ever quite as good as Hennen at relating to the faculty. What made John so successful was that he spent most of his time on the campuses meeting (and socializing with) faculty. They trusted him; therefore, faculty trusted that the ACA's primary interest was, as it was supposed to be, focused on the faculty. Those who held John's position after he left spent much of their time on ACA campuses visiting (and socializing) with the academic deans.[43]

The First Audit

When it was time for the ACA to have an audit, I called Mellon to ask if the ACA should hire a major auditing firm instead of a small local one. The answer was that if by hiring a local firm the ACA would save about $30,000—the amount of a year-long fellowship—I should hire locally. When I mentioned that I thought having a Coopers & Lybrand would give our Association more credibility, the Mellon representative said, "Your credibility comes from being funded by Mellon."

The first audit was conducted while the ACA employees were Eugene, John, and I. The first question the young accountant from a local firm asked was, "Explain to me how you pay bills." I said, "I open this drawer in this desk, take out this checkbook, and write a check." After a short pause, the auditor said that he supposed that with such a small staff, the ACA could not have multiple parties involved in paying bills to assure there was proper financial monitoring. When he learned that we did have an accountant who worked from her home part-time documenting what bills the ACA was paying, he suggested that person should be in the ACA office so that she could

---

43. Perhaps that is why some deans came to think, it seems, that the ACA was created to serve them.

quickly get answers to questions, such as whether travel was to be coded as related to a grant or as an office expense.

Then the auditor asked to see our personnel manual.

"Are you serious; there are three of us here."

"Well," he said, "at least let me see your policies governing vacation and sick days."

"When someone gets tired, he/she takes a vacation; when someone is sick, he/she stays home."

"With such policies you might give someone more vacation days than you give someone else.

"Yes," I replied, "it's called reward and punishment."

"No," he said, "it's called discrimination."

The Executive Committee and I spent much of the next year developing a personnel manual. So much time, in fact, that one of the presidents on the Executive Committee finally told me to let him know if the personnel manual was going to be on the agenda for a meeting so he could schedule a conflict for the date of that meeting.

Eugene went through all the personnel manuals from all the member colleges and listed every vacation, holiday, and benefit provided at each. I explained to her that we would not follow all the holidays and other benefits that any one of the colleges gave; we would just follow those that every college offered.

We hired Sonja Loftis, a recent honors graduate from Eastern KY University, as an in-house accountant. Kathryn Bowles, a student at Berea, helped with the administration of the grants, and Andrew Baskin was hired to work half-time overseeing the fellowship program while he maintained his position on the Berea College faculty on a half-time basis. Kathryn originally worked with us as a Berea College work-study student; after she graduated, she worked for a summer as an intern; then she worked as a full-time employee for the ACA until she left to work on her master's degree at UK. After completing her coursework at UK, she returned to work full-time at the ACA until shortly after I retired; then she left to work in the Office of Development at Centre College. Andrew left before I retired, when his daughter was old enough to attend college and Berea would not cover her tuition unless he was a full-time Berea College employee. Andrew later told me that he "missed the creative chaos of the ACA office." Sonja worked with the ACA for several years until she left to intern with a certified public accountant so she could qualify for the exam to be a CPA.

The national Elderhostel office in Boston was scrupulous about reporting expenditures related to the programs held and the money for the state offices. In 1993, when I told Bill Berkeley, president in the main office in Boston, that the KY Elderhostel office which had moved to UK from Eastern KY University was moving to Berea and would operate under the 501 (c) (3) classification of the ACA, Bill expressed concern about how carefully the money would be monitored. When I said that Mellon had just sent us a check for almost $3 million and they had not expressed any concerns about our ability to manage it, Bill's response was, "Mellon will take a budget report on the back of an envelope."[44] I couldn't argue with him at that point in

---

44. This was Bill Berkeley's opinion, not mine and, I suspect, not that of UK.

time since UK had been preparing budget reports (or at least editing mine) so I was not sure what Mellon's expectations were regarding reporting expenditures. The Elderhostel money continued to be managed by UK for about another year.

In 1994, when we received a grant from the National Science Foundation (NSF), I called Bill again and said, "NSF doesn't accept a budget report on the back of an envelope." He agreed, and the financial operations of the KY Elderhostel office were maintained by the ACA office until about 1999, when state offices were dissolved in favor of regional ones, and KY programs became part of the region headquartered in Atlanta. I had been state director of KY Elderhostel for twenty years. The ACA presidents did not complain at all about having to add twenty percent to my salary to cover the loss of the Elderhostel money; they seemed, I thought, relieved not to have KY Elderhostel as a program of the ACA. As one president pointed out to me, having the Elderhostel office at the ACA suggested that KY colleges, with my Elderhostel assignments related to them, were getting more attention than the colleges in the other four states in central Appalachia.

More about Staffing

While I was still at UK, I hired Sister Eileen O'Connor, who had offered Elderhostel programs at her convent, to assist me in running the state Elderhostel office and a recent UK graduate to develop and oversee programs hosted by UK. When the Berea office was established, Eileen continued to help with Elderhostel, and her vow of poverty meant her pay was basically for subsistence. The first full-time accountant I hired, Sonja Loftis, was willing to work for a nominal salary because her alimony payments would continue until her salary reached a certain level; John Hennen was not at all materialistic; and our multiple Berea College work-study students got paid less than minimum wage because some of their work offset tuition costs.

I was always surprised by the philosophy followed by many at the ACA colleges that dictated a new employee should make more than the person being replaced. My philosophy was to give an employee time to demonstrate his or her work ethic before raising them to a higher salary. I did not think people should be enticed to a job by the salary, but that I should reward someone who accepted a job and then proved to be better at it than the previous employee. When the board of ACA presidents decided that all raises, not just mine, needed to be approved by the Executive Committee of the board, I could raise salaries only slowly. After I retired, however, and most of the employees moved to positions at various colleges, it became clear that pay at the ACA was generous.

The board remained generous with my increases. One college president told me that he was confident he could easily find replacements for members of the ACA staff, but not for me. And benefits continued to be good, including health insurance;[45] dental care; and vacation, sick, and personal leave pay. Our retirement contributions were so high that I once had a call from one of the presidents asking how I had managed to secure such generous retirement contributions. I explained that the president who had drawn up my contract built in

---

45. I had originally assumed those of us in the ACA Berea office would be covered by the health insurance policy of Berea College with other benefits coming from the ACA. The Berea employment office put us on Berea's system. Several months later, I learned that only if we were on the Berea College payroll, not on that of the ACA, could we benefit from Berea's health insurance. Fortunately, there was a good Blue Cross/Blue Shield policy available to employees of associations and businesses with fewer than fifty employees.

the benefits of his employees; apparently, his retirement contributions were more generous than those at most other ACA colleges. At another time, one of the presidents at an ACA college told me after the end of a meeting of the Executive Committee that he would be willing to "grandfather in" current ACA employees to the existing benefits package, but he wanted new employees to receive fewer benefits. As we left the office, our new accountant turned to me and said, "Doesn't that change in benefits bother you?" "No," I said, "that request to change the benefits came after the meeting ended; there won't be any mention of it in the minutes so nobody here will even remember the suggestion at the next meeting." In fact, at the next meeting, not only did none of the presidents remember the issue about benefits being too high, but they also voted to add dental insurance to our benefit package.

I often said that my happiest time as a college administrator was when the office staff consisted of me and one assistant, but now I have to admit that the size of the staff is not so important as the camaraderie of all those in the office. I found that the larger the number of staff members, too often the more hostility tends to develop unless the head of the staff spends a lot of time nurturing good relationships.[46] With a lean staff, it was easy for each employee to realize his or her importance to the progress of the ACA. Each employee was fully committed to his or her project area, but each was also willing to work across the office. For example, when fellowship applications arrived, everyone gathered to make copies and package them to send to the Review Committee.

---

46. I was too impatient to do much nurturing, but my husband was great at it. Just ask my children. When my daughter tells me I'm a much better grandma than I was a mother, I tell her, "I did my part; I gave you a great father." And she agrees.

When annual reports were being prepared, everyone contributed expertise to the writing and designing of the reports.

So long as the number of staff remained low, it was easy to develop a strong sense of camaraderie. However, as the number of staff members increased to as high as fifteen (twelve full-time and three part-time) with every grant-funded project having its own staff and budget, when Tish Emerson came from Mellon to evaluate the ACA, she was critical of the fact that silos had developed across the ACA programs—one being the Central Library (overseen by Tony Krug from his home in TN), another being the technology projects (operating from a building on the Berea College campus), and a third being international study programs (administered by Fred Mullinax from his home in Lexington, KY). When a Writing-Across-the-Curriculum Project was funded and there was limited space in the ACA headquarters, Ed Welch, president at the University of Charleston in WV, offered the project director space on his campus. Of course, human resources and payroll and other financial functions, as well as the oversight of the core fellowship and scholarship programs, remained in Berea.

I understand why Tish did not like the idea that the ACA was made up of multiple programs which had become silos. Silos could leave each program so isolated from the others that a failure to communicate the work of each division across all programs might confuse people trying to understand the Association. Also, I suspect that the technology staff wondered why I did not spend more time raising money for them; and I know that one of my best employees wondered why I could not keep his program funded. Perhaps the silos did contribute to a sense among employees outside the main office in Berea that they were less cared about than those inside that office.

I always thought, however, that if one program needed extra staff it would be possible to shift some from another program—the one exception being the Central Library where few of us at the ACA could have stepped into the shoes of any of the employees there. The Library staff were located in the Berea office even though the project director worked a lot from his home and spent much of his time meeting with the librarians at their campuses. I assumed the director would spend more time in the Berea office if he needed to do so to cover the responsibilities of a staff person who might need to be out of the office for an extended period of time.

I disliked consultants who came and asked immediately for a meeting to discuss what outcome I was seeking. Typically, I wanted their ideas about what outcomes we might realistically expect. For example, we hired a marketing specialist to design some of our annual reports and redesign our letterhead stationery. When he wanted my ideas, my response was, "If I had such ideas, I wouldn't have needed to hire you. Give me your ideas and I'll tell you when I see one I like." When I commented on how much I liked working with consultants such as Pat Terenzini and Ernest Pascarella, who conducted a study of alumni from ACA colleges, Tish pointed out that they were not consultants, they were doing the work for me, not telling me how to do it. Indeed, that research would still not be completed if the two scholars had tried to teach me how to reach conclusions from the surveys.

For the most part, I had amazingly dedicated people working with me. Eugene Zita was the last assistant I had at UK, and her computer skills at the time were critical, given the fact that no one else in the office had even mastered Word. When the ACA office was established in Berea, I knew that having her continue to work with me would be a major asset.[47] She was incredible at anticipating my needs. I once landed at some remote airport in WV late one evening and realized there was no taxi in sight. Suddenly someone appeared from out of the darkness and asked, "Are you Dr. Brown?" Eugene had scheduled a driver to take me to the motel where I was staying.[48]

One of my "great mistakes" was moving Eugene from her position as my assistant to one where I could justify to the ACA board raising her salary beyond what they would approve for her work as an administrative assistant. I was naïve to assume she could do whatever job I gave her just because she was so good at taking care of me. I raised her to a staff position beyond her skill level. When one of the ACA presidents came to evaluate me one year, he insisted I fire Eugene if she did not want to return to being my assistant. And she didn't. After she left, she held a number of jobs which appeared menial but gave her the autonomy she wanted; she moved up to a position as manager of a local motel and has been there for several years.

J.P. Brantley, who had been a faculty member and the Elderhostel coordinator at Centre College, became an ACA Program Director and oversaw multiple funded projects. He was excellent in working with the academic deans but when the major grant he was overseeing ended, so did his position. By that time, most of the funding was

---

47. My favorite Eugene story is how she went into labor and was rushed to the hospital when I was out of town. When I returned to Lexington, I went to the hospital to see Eugene and the new baby. When I saw her, she handed me a stack of papers. She had brought a disk to the hospital and asked one of the nurses to print out the document on it because she had gone into labor before printing the document for me.

48. When I was traveling and would lose something, often my car keys, I would call Eugene. It never took her more than three guesses to determine where a lost item was. "Does the bedspread in your room have a floral print?" she asked. The keys were lying on that bed, hidden among the flowers on the spread.

targeted to the Central Library and projects supporting the use of technology, and each had its own project director. I had tried unsuccessfully to get him to identify one of his talents that we might find funding to support in a way that could benefit the faculty and/or students at our member colleges. I had learned from past experiences that people who had once been in charge of something did not work well when assigned to assist another project director.

I was always careful to explain to new employees that on grant money they could create their own futures by developing new ideas for programs that could be funded within their administrative areas or they could leave when the grants they were administering ended. I had learned early that if there was no outside funding for a project, the presidents were not likely to be willing to increase dues to cover the administrative costs associated with any staff position. Unfortunately, some people assumed I would raise money for projects they could administer if the one they had been administering could not be continued. It seemed no employee thought I would fire him/her; all seemed to think I would find a way to keep everyone. I suspect that my efforts to make every employee feel valued and to give each a lot of autonomy in setting his/her own work schedule led to some assuming I could not be callous enough to expect them to find another job if they had not done a good enough job for the foundation or other funding agency to continue their current one.[49]

It was so inconceivable that I might fire an employee that once

---

49. Once when the office was closed for Christmas, the UPS delivery truck arrived most days when I was the only one there. The driver finally said, "Are you the only one working this week?" I said, "Yes, I'm the only one making enough money to feel like I need to be working this week." His response was, "I thought you probably make a 'pretty penny.'"

when I went to the office of a relatively new employee to fire him, he assumed I was there for a very different purpose. I started by saying, "It is clear this is not the job you thought it would be, so let me help you find something else." He assumed I was going to write another grant to accommodate his skills and keep him at the ACA. When he realized that was not my intent, he called the chair of the ACA Governing Board and complained that I had misled him about what his responsibilities would be. Fortunately, the ACA presidents understood what they wanted from their boards, and generally treated me the way they wanted to be treated. In that case, the board chair replied to the disgruntled employee, "The board hired Alice and she hires all the other employees; the board does not get between the ACA president and employees she hires."

The ACA benefitted from numerous part-time and volunteer employees. When Dick Johnson from the Exxon Foundation retired, he and his wife moved to Berea for a semester and worked in the ACA office as volunteers. I hired Berea students in the summer when they were not enrolled at the college but wanted to stay in the area. But I also had occasional hires who did not understand the kind of commitment required to keep a program like the ACA raising millions of dollars each year to sustain or initiate opportunities for more than 3,000 faculty and more than 40,000 students. One person complained she was hired to work half-time, but she was working more than half-time. I couldn't be too sympathetic; many of the staff hired to work full-time were working more than full-time.

Everyone at the ACA except the clerical staff was on contract; few took advantage of the flexibility in scheduling their contract allowed, and most understood that ACA workshops or conferences were often held over weekends so that faculty attending would not miss the classes they were teaching. The only problem that concerned me regarding providing reasonable pay was related to travel time. While contract personnel usually understood that time spent traveling to various meetings and conferences was just part of their job responsibilities, I knew all too well how long days on the road could deplete not just time but also energy. We found an IRS policy regarding payment during hours on the road or in the air: when hourly employees were driving, they should be paid by the hours in transit; when they were just riding or flying, they were not entitled to pay during that time. We tried to compensate employees with release time after they had spent much of a week traveling whether they were driving or just napping in the back seat. And the office staff understood that for good cause they could get release time almost anytime. For example, when Kathryn was having trouble finishing her master's thesis, various people in the office covered her desk every afternoon for about six weeks so she could work on the thesis in the office. With two small kids at home, she wasn't making much progress there. I offered various staff members time off to take classes related to the technology or other skills they needed to be able to perform their office responsibilities.

Once Bob Watson from NSF overheard me talking with Rob Hoyt from the ACA computer program. Rob had called to tell me he really needed a generator for the servers that many of the ACA colleges were depending on for their computer services. I told him that I would work it into the budget on the next Mellon grant. He said he was having nightmares about waking up to find a snowstorm had cut off our electricity. "Okay," I said. "Buy the generator; I'll figure out how to pay for it later." After Rob hung up, Bob said, "You're the kind of boss I wish I had; just let me tell you what I need and you'll figure out how to pay for it."

Multiple business executives, such as Reed Hastings, CEO of Netflix, have preached that if you "hire slowly and fire quickly,"[50] you can increase the "talent density" of your organization. My problem was that when I had funding for a new position, I was always in a hurry to find someone to fill it and get started fulfilling the obligations to which I had committed. But the weaknesses of new hires always became clear early in their term at the ACA, so I tried to fire quickly. The one time that proved to be impossible was when the employee's response was that she could not do her work because she was being sexually harassed; I quickly learned that it is illegal to fire someone making that claim until you have proved it is not true—a process that can be long and create distress across the office.

The employee who complained she "couldn't do her job" because another employee was "sexually harassing" her was a relatively new employee; she was accusing a long-time employee who was respected for his dignity and diligence. It was hard to imagine him sexually harassing anything. The ACA lawyer said that I had to question every other employee to learn if others felt such harassment, and that I could not do anything that could be interpreted as discriminating against the person complaining: I had to give her the same raises as I gave others, the same promotions, etc. One afternoon shortly after her complaint (and before I questioned any other employee), I met with her at a restaurant outside the office to discuss the problem privately; I asked her what she wanted me to do—short of firing the person accused—to protect her from feeling harassed. I don't

---

50. Dr. Bowen's words are similar: "Plan carefully, then execute rapidly." Quoted from "William G. Bowen, Princeton Educator Who Championed Poor and Minority Students, Dies at 83," an article in *The New York Times* by Sam Roberts, Oct. 21, 2016.

remember what she suggested, if anything, but the next morning, I found her letter of resignation on my desk, along with the housewarming present I had given her.[51] She never came back to the office; we mailed her final check to her.

One new ACA employee phoned me one Sunday to tell me she could not go to the conference she was supposed to be hosting in WV because it was snowing there. "And that is why you should have gone yesterday," I replied. She understood that she might need to work on some weekends, but she never expected to have to "give up all of a weekend."[52] What I learned was that my best employees were ones who had worked with the ACA as work-study students or who had worked with me in other settings before the ACA because they knew what I expected and were willing to keep up with my expectations. And, of course, Berea students could appreciate what the ACA was doing for those from a background of poverty and inadequate educational opportunities. The fact that faculty who received ACA benefits were so grateful made it hard for those of us working at the ACA not to recognize the importance of our work and be dedicated to it.

I should never give short shrift to the multiple Berea College undergraduates who served as work-study students in our office. We had the luxury of sending those that did not meet our expectations back to the campus; most exceeded our expectations. One young student was answering phones at the ACA when someone called and asked

---

51. It may seem that I fired a lot of employees, but the only ones I fired are mentioned in this memoir; those who quit are not included here but most left for better jobs. There was not a lot of turnover until my retirement; almost every employee left shortly after I retired.

52. All the faculty scheduled to participate in the conference beginning on Sunday were able to get to the conference site—many by leaving their homes on Saturday.

for me. "She's not in the office," he said. The caller responded: "She left early since it's Friday afternoon?" The student knew the right answer even though I had never given it to him: "She would never do that."

New Facilities

Within a year after the move from UK, it was clear that the ACA office space was too small, so we moved from the second-floor apartment to the second floor of a house built early in the 1900s. Berea College had bought the house, added a large parking lot, and rented it to various retailers. The space on that second floor included four offices, a small workroom, and a bath. When the gift shop on the main floor of the house closed and the space there became available, we rented the whole house, including an entrance hall, a board room, a closed-in back porch, two offices, a large workroom, and a basement we could use to store archived materials (so long as we kept them off the floor which routinely flooded). While the ACA Governing Board balked a bit at more than doubling the costs associated with adding the space, my response was that although we really did not need that much room at the time, it would not be long before we would need the space and by then it probably would not be available. My comments didn't impact the presidents as much as the one by Sonja, our accountant at the time: "Paying more for rent will help justify an increase in our federal overhead rate."

We were in that house on Chestnut Street until I retired. Although there was no central air and periodically a ceiling tile would fall in the workroom, the house had the charm of many older homes, with a wrap-around front porch, lots of trees in the yard, a fireplace, large windows in every room, and oak trim throughout. The location of the house was great; it was across from the Berea College Log House (gift shop) and near the town square where several restaurants, the bookstore, and Boone Tavern (the college hotel) were located.[53] But my affinity for old houses was not shared by those who replaced me.

Within six years after I had retired, there were fewer than a dozen ACA college presidents who had been part of the organization when I was president. And whenever I heard from someone at the ACA, I was always surprised by what I learned. When the chief financial officer, who was also serving as acting president of the ACA, called to tell me the ACA had a $3 million surplus from "grant residuals," I said that there was no such thing: if money remains after a project has ended, you must return the money or ask for an extension of the project. He explained that when one of the Mellon grants ended with $7,000 remaining in the budget, Mellon had said he could use it for anything he wanted. I asked, "How many $7,000 residuals did it take to make $3 million?" I realized the money was from Mellon, one of the last grants I received when I was ACA president for supporting faculty projects that involved collaboration enhanced by using technology. I was also surprised by the fact that none of the amount originally awarded had been spent, suggesting that not much information or promotion of the opportunities available had been distributed. Also, there was no mention of how much interest had been earned during the six or so years the funding had been invested.

---

53. When I returned to the campus for a meeting in 2019, I went to Berea Coffee and Tea, a block from the ACA office. The owner, whom I had not seen for at least ten years, recognized me immediately. He said, "I remember you." I said, "Do you remember what I drink?" He said, "Chai tea, and you were always in a hurry."

The annual meeting of the presidents was approaching and one vote to be taken was related to using the $3 million "residual" to construct an office building for the ACA staff. I called one of the long-time presidents to ask him about this plan to build a building with money awarded for faculty projects. He assured me the presidents would never approve that. Then, they did approve it. The person who had assured me the board would never approve using money awarded for faculty to build an office explained that the new presidents had outvoted those who had been at the ACA long enough to know how inappropriate it was for the ACA to build a new building—especially if it was being built with money awarded for projects identified by the faculty.[54] And apparently no one spent much time analyzing the figures that showed that a new building of about 10,000 square feet could be operated at a cost less than the office (about 2,000 square feet) in Berea—the argument the financial officer had made to justify the new building.

Later, I heard from one of the long-time ACA college presidents that when Mellon was asked to change the purpose of the three-million-dollar grant, the response was, "Use the money for the building if that is what you think you need, but don't ever come back to us again." By this time, presidents and program officers at multiple foundations that had supported the ACA for decades had asked me why they had not received reports and/or could not get information from appeals they made to the ACA. But losing the ongoing funding from a foundation that had contributed for over thirty years—and had contributed almost

---

54. Later one of the presidents called to console me about the decision to build an office building. He said, "But if you have ever dreamed about a bunch of old men sitting around a parking lot talking about how much they miss you, your dream has come true." That wasn't much consolation, but it was a kind gesture.

$40 million in some fifty grants—was a major blow to the progress of the ACA and the colleges supported. That amount included grants funded by Mellon at the ACP and at the ACA.

The acting president of the ACA had told me that the reason the Mellon program officer had told him not to apply for their funding in the future was that the foundation was not going to fund consortia any longer. Later I realized that did not appear to be true; a look at the website of other regional consortia (such as the Associated Colleges of the South) indicated that Mellon had continued funding consortia. Mellon had funded the Appalachian College Program at UK for three years before I was the director of it and for roughly ten years after I was director. Mellon funded the ACA under my leadership for fifteen years, and in most of those years, as I remember them, the grants from Mellon were more frequent and larger than in previous years. There were lots of reasons to believe that since Mellon clearly wanted to assist the thirty-five or so colleges that were members and giving to the ACA was their way of doing that, funding from that foundation would have continued at some level for decades longer.

In The Mellon Foundation's annual report for 2009, the year after I retired, the new president of that foundation, Don Randel, wrote about the 2008 market decline. Responding to the question about what the foundation would do considering the financial situation, he said, "In the end, we can only continue to do what we have long done—help a rather small fraction of the 4,000 institutions of higher education in the country maintain a commitment to activities that we have always cared about." Yet, by 2019, when Mellon produced a history of the first fifty years of the work of the foundation, the ACA received only a few lines of recognition:

The Appalachian College Association (1990-2008)

In the 1970s, Mellon became a major funder of colleges in the Appalachian region, one of the nation's poorest. Following a first major effort to support faculty and curriculum development in 1978, the Foundation made the first of two rounds of funding in the following year to bring faculty members in the humanities at small liberal arts colleges in the region to the Appalachian Center at the University of Kentucky, where they could conduct summer research. The success of this endeavor ultimately attracted other funding that, together with another grant from Mellon, established the Appalachian College Association.[55]

The Foundation didn't acknowledge the multiple other grants from Mellon that enabled the ACA to benefit faculty across the region for decades.

How to Become a President

I should mention how I went from being the executive director of the ACA to being the president. When John Chandler wrote the report about the program at UK, he was serving as president of the Association of American Colleges and Universities (AAC&U). He invited me to attend the annual meeting of the AAC&U without paying a registration fee. At that meeting, I saw a couple of ACA academic deans, but there was little I found relevant in the program except a lunch meeting for presidents and foundation officers. I attended that meeting, met several foundation officers, and took notes regarding applications I could make.

---

55. "The Mellon Foundation at Fifty, Part IV: Expanding Access to Higher Education, Humanities, and the Arts." *2019 Annual Report.*

A year or so later, I paid the registration fee and attended the annual AAC&U meeting, but when I started into the luncheon with foundation officers, I was stopped. My name tag indicated I was an executive director. I tried to explain that I was representing thirty-seven[56] college presidents who were not present, but I was told that the luncheon was for presidents themselves, not their representatives. When I returned to the ACA office, I wrote the Executive Committee and said I needed a new title. After I was named president, I never had any trouble getting into the room with other presidents and foundation officers at the AAC&U—or at the Council of Independent Colleges (CIC)—meetings.

But I never let the title of president confuse me when I experienced how the ACA college presidents viewed me. Just before I was about to move to Berea to set up the new ACA office, I had a call from one of the ACA presidents. Eugene (my assistant at UK) transferred the call to me. I was feeling honored to know that college presidents would be calling me. Then I learned that he was calling to ask me to pick up a pair of his wife's shoes that she had left in Lexington and bring them to the upcoming ACA meeting. Years later, when someone announced at the presidents' annual meeting that I had laryngitis, one of the presidents loudly spoke up to say, "There is a god." Clearly, the presidents, at least many of them, did not see me as a president. Occasionally, one of the presidents would remind me that I "had never been a president." Tish once told me I should reply by saying, "And you've never been the president of a consortium of thirty-five colleges."

---

56. The number of colleges in the ACA at that time.

When Mary Patterson McPherson (Pat) became vice president at Mellon, she and Tish came to Kentucky so I could introduce her to some of the ACA presidents and deans and fellowship recipients. We spent several days traveling across the region to attend gatherings of the presidents, deans and beneficiaries of the Mellon funding. After several of these receptions, Pat, who had served for twenty years as president of Bryn Mawr College before serving at Mellon, said, "I haven't met any of your women presidents."

"That's because we don't have any," I replied.

"Why not?"

"People in Appalachia don't think of women as leaders."

"But they obviously think of you as a leader," Pat said with a look of disbelief.

"No, they don't; they think of me as a glorified administrative assistant."

"But," Pat said, "they are always talking about how much work you get done."

Tish spoke up: "Yes, that's what the administrative assistants do: they get the work done."

Strategic Plan

After a few years of operating in Berea, the ACA was raising between $1 million and $5 million each year. In the first four years at the Berea office, the ACA received five grants totaling $8 million from Mellon alone. Working on advice from Tish Emerson, who pointed out that funding the same program for over twenty years was not a model Mellon was likely to endorse regardless of how successful it was, I submitted a proposal to the National Endowment for the Humanities (NEH) for a Challenge Grant to develop an endowment for the fellowship program. The fellowships at UK that John Stephenson had named to honor James Still had been endowed by Mary Bingham. Interest earned was being used to support graduates of ACA member colleges attending graduate programs at UK.

When the ACA became an independent association, the fellowships in the humanities and sciences were named the Stephenson Fellowships. I contacted John's daughter and asked her to write the proposal to NEH since she had worked as a grant writer for several agencies. All I had to do was find documentation to verify the success of the program. That was an easy assignment; not only did we have information on every dissertation or book that had been written by a fellowship recipient, but we also had the list of awards made every year since the first fellowship was awarded in 1980.[57]

Shortly after that submission to NEH, I received a call from a program officer there saying, "We have everything we need to submit your proposal to the reviewers—except your latest strategic plan." I responded, "We were just about to do one." She said, "You have three months; I need it by the first of June." I called the Executive Committee and said that we should hire a consultant; and I mentioned three people I thought could do a good job on the assignment. To my surprise, they chose the only woman on the list—Beth Baxter, who had

---

57. One year, Tish Emerson called and told me Bill Bowen wanted to meet me the next time I was in New York. I asked, "Why?" She said, "He just thinks he should know the person he gave $6 million this year." I said, "But what if he wants to take it back after he meets me?" She said, "We won't let him do that."

helped draft proposals for various ACA projects related to bringing the colleges up to date with technology. AT&T had recommended her as a consultant years before when that company was donating computers to UK for the ACP to distribute to member colleges.

Eight presidents and four academic deans served as the Steering Committee for the Strategic Plan. The opportunities they identified were related to the possibilities for offering grants to faculty in professional fields; sharing resources in such areas as curriculum and technology; bringing special resources to each campus, such as technology experts; increasing opportunities for study abroad and internships for students; and approaching more governmental agencies for federal funding. Threats included competition from public institutions; the inability to keep pace with new technologies; the isolation and socio-economic culture of Appalachia; and the changing priorities for funding agencies.

Beth interviewed every ACA president (most in person but a few by email and phone) and then looked at what would be in the best interest of the most member colleges. While some presidents complained that Beth had not considered their suggestions, she offered recommendations that addressed concerns of most of those responding. Addressing concerns about dues, Beth recommended that the ACA office should track the financial benefits to each college: amounts awarded directly to faculty for fellowships and travel grants plus the value of other experiences. For example, if a faculty member attended a conference the ACA sponsored, the person's expenses, such as housing and mileage, and a percentage of the cost of the program (speakers, space, supplies, etc.) would be included among financial benefits acquired by that member college.

The first year we made that calculation, the results revealed that for every dollar a member college paid in dues, the college received at least seven dollars in benefits. Joel Cunningham, from the University of the South, was the only institutional leader to comment on what "a good deal" the ACA offered. He said that if the ACA could promise him that return on every dollar paid to the ACA, he would want to raise dues as high as possible. The one year that I found a college had not gotten more in benefits than the institution had paid in dues, I called the president of that college and said I was worried the ACA was not serving his college very well. His response was, "Our library burned last year, and the head of the ACA Central Library, Tony Krug, worked with our staff and the architects building a new library. Tony's consultancy alone was worth more than the dues our college paid." Most of the ACA presidents, however, complained about every fifty-cent increase in the per-student dues even though the benefits-to-dues ratio increased for most of the colleges throughout my tenure at the ACA.[58]

The second major recommendation Beth Baxter made was that the ACA should recruit an Advisory Council. What Beth had noticed in interviewing college presidents was that each could focus only on the needs of his or her institution, and usually those needs were related to a very local need, such as renovation of buildings. She suggested that we should have a group of leaders in higher education look across the member colleges and focus on how the ACA could address common needs, not ones of a few individual campuses. Even the issue of renovations was once considered. Rick Kneipper from Jones Day in Dallas, TX, who had helped the ACA develop an intellectual property policy,

---

58. See Appendix C for a list indicating benefits received for dues paid from 1990 to 2008.

spoke to the ACA Executive Committee about having one firm oversee dormitory renovations across multiple campuses. The objection of the Executive Committee at the time was that the firm being promoted was based in Texas, not Appalachia; but no one followed-up on the idea that some architectural firm in Appalachia might like to oversee such an effort.

About a year after the recommendation that the ACA needed an Advisory Council, I brought up the suggestion at the annual meeting of the presidents. One of the presidents said, "If you think you need an Advisory Council, get one." I asked that each president send me the name of a nominee for the Council. When I had not received even one name at the end of the semester, Tish Emerson and I made a list of people who we thought would be strong assets for the ACA; many had ties to major funding agencies, such as Edgar Beckham, who had served at the Ford Foundation, and Robert Watson, who was director of NSF's Division of Undergraduate Education; two were leading other regional consortia—Elizabeth Hayford of the Associated Colleges of the Midwest and Wayne Anderson from the Associated Colleges of the South; one was a Washington correspondent for the *Los Angeles Times* and editor of the *Encyclopedia of Appalachia*. When I sent the list to the presidents, I said that it contained the names of those nominated and if there was anyone on the list any of the presidents considered inappropriate, I needed to know that. The only person any president indicated as someone inappropriate for a role advising the ACA was a woman who had held a major administrative position at UK and then became president of a well-known private college in the Northeast.

Everyone invited agreed to serve on the new Advisory Council. There was a core group that attended every annual meeting from the time they joined the Council until my retirement; others who accepted the invitation to be on the Council seemed to think that all the ACA needed from them was the use of their names, and they were only on the Council for a year or two.

The Council was an incredible resource to me for the rest of the time I led the ACA. Members attended the annual meetings of the ACA college presidents, notified me of new priorities for various funders, became advocates for the academic deans,[59] and gave me a new perspective on what was possible for a regional consortium. Most attended my retirement event, and I arranged a private meeting for them with the new ACA president, Paul Chewning. It came as a real surprise to me to learn that the new ACA president never contacted any of the Council members after he took office. As one Council member told me, they were left to conclude for themselves that the Advisory Council no longer existed.

Other recommendations included seeking new sources of funding to include all disciplines, not just arts and sciences, in the fellowship program. McCune, a foundation in Pittsburgh, and other donors endowed the Jean Ritchie Fellowships for faculty in the performing arts and the Wilma Dykeman Fellowships in professional fields, such as education and business. The sources of funding increased every year, and as new projects were funded staff were added. The size of the ACA staff grew to as large as fifteen at one point, with five basic staff in permanent positions funded primarily by dues: president, administrative assistant, chief finance officer, director of the Central

---

59. Edgar Beckham, who had been a program officer at the Ford Foundation, chose to mentor the academic deans. Once at a meeting of the deans' council, when he heard me say that I was a "product" person, not a "process" person, he said, "And I consider myself one of your products."

Library, and an accountant. Shortly before I retired, Mellon endowed a position for vice president of programs, assuring that the new president would be able to devote most of his or her time to fundraising.[60]

Of course, these counts of ACA employees never included the Berea College staff who provided security, general maintenance, and care of the grounds around our building—the sort of employees who are seldom seen so we often take their services for granted. One practice suggested to me by the wife of a former UK president was hosting a Thanksgiving lunch for all the service providers not being directly paid by the ACA, including the mailman and the UPS delivery person, as well as the lawn keepers, those from the physical plant,[61] the folks from printing, and those providing other such services. The first year or so there seemed to be some reluctance on the part of such staff to come into our office for a meal, but after that they began to bring friends who worked with them but whom we might not have known to invite.

Competition in Fundraising

Within a year after I retired, I had heard from many of those who had once generously funded the ACA that the ACA had returned money and told one donor not to send more money and spent money for purposes outside those related to the original

---

60. It seems clear that Mellon expected the ACA to continue raising money, and Mellon continued funding for the Central Library and study at the Salzburg Institute for several years after I retired.

61. Such as those who came to replace fallen ceiling tiles and burned-out light bulbs and to wash the windows.

mission of the ACA.⁶² I speculated that the presidents told Paul they didn't want him to maintain the relationships with potential funders because ACA efforts could create obstacles to fundraising efforts of their staff.⁶³ In fact, when an officer at Mellon asked me why I had left and why they had not heard anything from the new president, I defended Paul: "It was time for me to leave, and my replacement is probably following advice from some of the presidents; they don't want him raising money because they think he might interfere with their efforts to raise money." During my presidency, occasionally someone would suggest that raising money should not be a priority for the ACA, but there was never any discussion that led to a mandate not to raise money and there was always a list of how to spend it.

Even a president at Berea⁶⁴ had suggested a committee of ACA presidents should be charged with identifying where and for what the ACA president should be allowed to fundraise. Danielle Carr-Ramdath, a Mellon program officer, was attending the meeting of presidents when

---

62. Presidents or staff at several foundations asked me at various points after I retired, "What happened to the ACA?" They complained they couldn't get reports from the office. The NY Community Trust was told not to send more money to the ACA because the staff couldn't find students interested in having an internship. Grants for international study and community service ended, and it seems the ACA had not asked any funders of such experiences for new grants. Apparently, the grants for student scholarships from NSF also ended without applications for renewals.

63. Initially, when I began developing proposals to send to potential funding sources after my move to Berea, I contacted every president in the Association to ask if there were any objections to the requests I planned to make. It was only Maryville College, near the Alcoa Company in TN, that responded, saying I should not approach Alcoa.

64. This was the president concerned that people contributing to the ACA might have thought they were giving to Berea College because the ACA was housed on Berea's campus. Only once did someone call me to talk about making a donation, and I quickly realized he wanted to contribute to Berea College. I gave him the number to Berea's development office, and then said, "But if you ever want to give to thirty-five private colleges in Appalachia, call me back."

he made that comment; she said, "You don't want to interfere with Alice's autonomy when she is fundraising." Then, the president's question was, "Is that your opinion or Mellon's?" Danielle's response was, as she stared directly into the president's eyes: "In this room, I am Mellon." Limiting my fundraising was not ever discussed after that meeting.

The idea that the ACA's fundraising interfered with that of the member colleges never seemed realistic to me. The ACA did not ask individuals for money (except when fellowship recipients were solicited during the endowment campaign) and the Association didn't ask small, local foundations for funding. The foundations and federal agencies that funded the ACA were unlikely to have funded any of the ACA colleges directly, except for Berea, Sewanee, Emory & Henry, and one or two others. The Mellon Foundation, for example, tended to fund liberal arts colleges that had at least 1,000 students but fewer than 5,000, and had more than seventy-five percent of its graduates in arts and science disciplines. Bob Watson from NSF asked me to apply for funding that helped multiple member colleges since so few of the colleges could qualify on their own. It seems obvious that any large foundation would rather give to one nonprofit that could then distribute the funds to thirty-five small colleges (or some subset of the whole) and monitor the work funded across those colleges. Our fundraising was also helped by the fact that every college in the ACA (except for Sewanee) served primarily students from disadvantaged populations in a region where education was one of the last hopes for lifting people out of poverty.

Ellen Burbank at Pew once referred to funding the ACA as "wholesale awarding of grants." At that time, Pew was our major funder, and I overhead Ellen tell someone from Mellon that fact; the response from the program officer at Mellon was, "You may have given them the most, but we gave to them first." One foundation representative told me that he would be happy to come to meet with me during the annual gathering of the ACA presidents—but only if he didn't have to talk to any of the presidents. The idea of talking with one person versus thirty-five is attractive on many levels. And, as Martha Perry (from the McCune Foundation) said at my retirement dinner, "You could depend on Alice to tell you the truth; if a project wasn't working as planned, she would let you know. Some program directors think that grant makers only want to hear about the 'good stuff.'" Duncan McBride from NSF talked about the fact that I kept him informed about the work of the ACA even when the ACA didn't have funding from NSF; I wouldn't let him forget about the needs of the ACA colleges. There were many reasons that charitable organizations wanted to help the ACA. One might have been to get me "off their backs."

At one point well into my term as ACA president, the Executive Committee of the ACA board created a task force on the future of the Association. Tom Morris, president at Emory & Henry at that time, was chair with two other presidents, two academic deans, and one member of the Advisory Committee. There were three scenarios for the future of the ACA. First, dues should be increased to cover at least seventy percent of administrative costs for "core" operations: "faculty fellowships and travel grants, student grants for research, and the library program." The committee seemed to think that the need for fundraising would be eliminated as the ACA evolved into an association fully supported by the member colleges.[65] A second possibility

---

65. There was no explanation of where the other thirty percent of the cost of administration for core programs would come from if the ACA was not going to be raising new money except the suggestion that the endowment could cover part of the costs for administration. This suggestion did not take into consideration that the endowment had been established with no mention of administrative costs (except for costs associated with meetings of the fellowship review committee), and changing the endowment agreement

was having a two-tiered membership dues structure where some colleges would pay higher dues to support fundraising by the association and only those colleges paying the higher rate could benefit from new programs supported by the new grants. The third option was including "fundraising" or "development" as one of the "core" programs and making related costs part of the core budget. There seems to have been no presentation to the full board for a vote to implement any of the recommendations. Perhaps I should not have asked John Stephenson to include all the private colleges in the five states of central Appalachia in the ACA instead of just the "strong" ones. The "strong" ones were not the loudest voices among those complaining about the success of the ACA in raising funds.

Sustaining Projects

One of the major chores for ACA employees and beneficiaries of ACA funding was maintaining a level of excellence for each project so that the agencies that had funded those projects would want to continue their support, and others would want to join the early contributors. What follows are some problems that complicate maintaining an image that encourages current funders to continue funding and new funders to start funding.

What the college faculty never seemed to realize was how much time was invested in impressing potential funders. Faculty attending the annual Technology Summit complained about luncheon speakers such as Jim Clayton, who built Clayton Mobile Homes into a business that

would be a major undertaking.

he sold to Berkshire Hathaway for $1.7 billion. When I heard the complaints, I pointed out that Clayton was not there to entertain or impress the ACA faculty and staff; the faculty and staff were there to impress Clayton. I wanted him to help support the ACA and projects like the Summit. By the end of his presentation, it was clear that those in the audience had not really enjoyed his appearance, and the way he and his crew quickly left the building without speaking to anyone (including me as I was following him out) made it clear he had not been impressed by the audience. Other speakers the attendees at the ACA conferences did not like were those associated with state or federal offices.

It wasn't that those of us at the ACA never made a mistake or overlooked a report deadline, but when we did fall short of expectations, we made every effort to rectify the problem. My assistant called to confirm plans for each major speaker's presentation at the ACA meetings; she once asked me if our speakers were not grown people who were perfectly capable of maintaining their own schedules and showing up where they were expected and when they were expected. While her point was well taken, the fact remains that even careful, dependable people sometimes fail to fulfill the expectations of others. And I didn't want the keynote speaker for an audience of over 400 faculty to fail to fulfill his commitment.

One frustration I had at the ACA was trying to get the faculty designing workshops or seminars to involve widely recognized speakers in their sessions. Their inclination was to invite faculty at other member colleges to serve as leaders in every session—or to invite the same good speakers they had heard at last year's event—which would have been a good idea if it were not for the fact that it was mainly the same ACA faculty who attended every year.

This tendency of having many of the faculty involved in ACA events repeating the experiences of past years was the problem Robert Zemsky spoke of when he pointed out that the ACA needed more new faculty from the various member colleges to attend ACA events. For example, we prided ourselves on the fact that about 400 people attended the Summit every year, including primarily faculty but also students who had received Ledford grants and academic deans. But it was usually the same faculty among the 400 participants who came when there were over 3,000 faculty across the ACA. And, as Zemsky noted when he spoke to a group of faculty at another ACA event, "Most of you attending here are near fifty or older; you need to be encouraging the new faculty on your campuses to attend." They may have wanted, as one faculty member suggested, "to keep the ACA to themselves," but that was hardly a way to assure the continued existence of the ACA.

Just as it is important to keep the priorities of funders in mind when writing the first grant to them, it is just as important to follow their recommendations when the time has come to prepare for a continuation grant. Following is an experience illustrating the importance of paying close attention to the program officers or other representatives of foundations who are considering funding your organization or continuing to fund you after their current grant has ended.

Each fall, the ACA hosted a tour of ACA colleges for program officers from foundations and other agencies funding the ACA, and program officers from foundations we hoped would fund the ACA. This was my way of having funders who seemed pleased by the work of the ACA to encourage others to follow their example. A major new initiative developed when one of the people invited to a fall tour—Linda Jacobs from Culpeper—offered to entertain a proposal related to writing across the curriculum. The result was a three-year grant of almost $500,000 for a program designed to develop a focus on writing across all the disciplines at each college.

We hired a bright new Ph.D. who had just completed her dissertation at WVU on teaching writing in engineering programs—Sati Boggs. Since office space in the ACA building in Berea was full at the time, and Sati's husband was working in WV, the University of Charleston in WV offered to provide an office and some staff assistance for Sati, but Sati also had to teach two classes each semester for the English Department at that university. Keeping the faculty in the UC English Department happy on a day-to-day basis and keeping the faculty across multiple ACA colleges happy on a semester-by-semester basis was a stressful assignment, but Sati managed to do both exceptionally well.[66]

Just a year before the Culpeper grant was to end, I had a call from Linda. She said that Culpeper was going to merge with the Rockefeller Brothers Fund, and if I wanted an extension of the current grant, I needed to get a proposal to her within the next two weeks. Linda and I talked about the Student Technology Assistants (STAs) and how that model could be used to develop Student Writing Assistants (SWAs).[67] I called Beth Baxter, who had written several grants for the ACA, and several faculty from colleges participating in the current project and asked them to meet to write the grant for Culpeper. I explained

---

66. When the participants in the Writing-Across-the-Curriculum Project attended a conference at Cornell University, they grew anxious about their presentation when they realized faculty from Harvard were also presenting. After the conference, several of the Harvard participants indicated they were very impressed by the collaborative spirit across the ACA colleges; at Harvard it's "every boat on its own bottom." That comment cemented the commitment of the ACA program participants to the writing program.

67. SWAs could be junior or senior students who excelled in courses requiring significant writing expertise. Each SWA would be assigned to a freshman or sophomore class to help students with their writing assignments.

the Student Writing Assistants idea to Beth, and she met with the selected faculty most of the day. The proposal produced was basically a continuation of what the first grant from Culpeper had provided. When I asked Beth about the Writing Assistants idea, she said simply, "The faculty didn't want to do that; they just wanted help to continue the current writing programs." But the foundation did not want to fund a continuation of the previous grant; few foundations do want to fund extensions of programs they previously funded unless there is some new element added to those programs.

The new proposal kept the existing goals in place, such as covering expenses for faculty to attend conferences and develop writing centers on their campuses. By the time I saw the proposal, it was too late for me to revise it; and if I had gotten a grant to train students to assist other students with writing skills, the faculty were likely to have resisted participating in it. I should have followed one of my main instincts—ask for money for what the funding agencies are funding—and made that philosophy clear to Beth and the faculty working with her. I was not surprised to get a call from Linda, who was not at all pleased by the proposal submitted and resented the fact that I had taken her time to identify work that might have been funded and then submitted a request for more funding of the current work. I regretted not taking the time to help the faculty team write a proposal that incorporated at least some new aspects into an extension of what they were already doing.

Fortunately, there was enough interest in the writing program to continue it for a while, even after Culpeper funding ended—until Sati learned she was pregnant with twins. Once again, a lesson was clear: in order to thrive, a program needs a devoted, competent, energetic leader. And finding a replacement for Sati seemed impossible. Once again, a project important to several ACA colleges ended when there was no outside funder to subsidize the small amount the colleges might pay—even though no skill is more important to college graduates than the ability to write well.

The lesson learned was that when someone from a funding source is willing to talk with you and offer suggestions, pay close attention. It is especially important if a foundation or federal agency representative offers suggestions, to either use them or wait to submit a proposal until you are ready to incorporate the recommendations. Don't ask for assistance and then ignore the advice.

Building an Endowment for Fellowships and Grants

When the ACA was in the middle of developing a request for an NEH Challenge grant, I visited the office in Washington to meet the program officers and talk about how the ACA planned to administer the grant. The grant requested was about a million dollars and the match required was three million dollars, which my Mellon program officer had suggested the Foundation might provide. When I told the folks at NEH, Fred Winter and Barbara Ashbrook, that Mellon would probably provide the match, they pointed out that the purpose of a Challenge Grant was to broaden an organization's base of support. I responded that the ACA did not have a large base of support; we had a few foundations that funded us generously. Barbara pointed out that most Challenge Grant recipients ask their alumni to contribute. I pointed out that the ACA alumni were faculty at small private colleges who had benefitted from a fellowship; most made about $30,000 to $40,000 per year in their teaching positions. "But,"

I added, "I will ask them." Barbara asked why I thought Mellon would give us the matching funds. I said that Mellon had been funding our program for about twenty years, and if they thought they could give us three million dollars and never see us again, they would jump at the chance.

The head of the Appalachian Center at Berea College had told me about the Challenge Grant program, and he submitted a proposal for Berea at the same time as I submitted one for the ACA. When Berea's proposal was rejected[68] and the ACA's proposal was funded, we had another example of how a proposal offering assistance for faculty at thirty-five colleges was more competitive than one, perhaps even one better written, that would benefit faculty from only one college. The grant from NEH was $600,000, the most awarded to any project that year, so the match required only $1,800,000. But we were determined to raise as much as possible so we could award as many fellowships as possible.

When I wrote to all the previous fellowship recipients, over sixty percent made a contribution. The total amount collected from them was about $22,000, but the Mellon trustees, I was told, were greatly impressed by the show of support reflected by the large number of contributions from beneficiaries of the fellowship program. Various foundations that had been funding the ACA also made contributions. Although $2.4 million was the initial total raised for fellowships for faculty in the humanities, contributions for fellowships in other disciplines were also significant.

Contributions from McCune and others supported newly named fellowships in fine and performing arts (Jean Ritchie Fellowships) and those in professional fields, such as education or nursing (Wilma

---

68. Later, Berea's request was also funded.

Dykeman Fellowships). A high percentage of the fellowships need to be awarded to faculty in the humanities because the NEH grant of $600,000 and the match of $1.8 million (for the total of $2.4 million) were expected to reflect the minimum of the endowment for humanities faculty. Part of the funding from Mellon and individuals was designated as endowment for science faculty, and fellowships in the arts (humanities) **and** sciences were named to honor John Stephenson, the founder of the fellowship program. His wife, Jane, made a major contribution. While NEH staff indicated the agency would not examine annual reports about awards to determine if a certain percentage had been awarded for research in the humanities, if the ACA ever returned for additional funding from NEH, the ACA would have to show an appropriate number of awards had benefitted humanities faculty.

When the campaign was completed, the ACA had a long list of new donors. Four local banks contributed; the Hanes Foundation, which had never before contributed, sent a check for $25,000; Hirtle-Callahan, the firm managing the endowment, contributed; one hundred percent of the ACA staff contributed; most of the ACA presidents made personal contributions and each college contributed $30,000 to fulfill a requirement for matching funds. One member of the Advisory Council gave $1,000. William Friday, who had retired as Chancellor of UNC-Chapel Hill and was then director of the Kenan Foundation, approved a contribution of $100,000—after Otis Singletary, at that time recently retired as president of UK and a friend of Chancellor Friday, flew to NC to ask for a contribution. I understand that Singletary said to Friday, "If I were sitting in your chair, and you were sitting in mine, I'd give **you** the money."[69]

---

69. Since I am working primarily from memory, I apologize if I have omitted any major contributor.

We raised more than was needed to match the NEH money and received additional funds for fellowships for faculty in the sciences, professional fields, and arts.[70] But the reality of what an endowment income will fund came as a shock to me. I once (probably more than once) remarked to a Mellon program officer that if the Foundation would just endow our fellowships, we would not have to come back every three years asking for more funding. Then, when Mellon did contribute generously to the endowment for the fellowships, the first year we needed to depend on income from the endowment there was a major drop in the stock market. I realized that with only about $100,000 of interest having been earned, we would be able to award only a few fellowships; and knowing how many faculty who were likely to apply would have low self-confidence and, if rejected, were likely to say, "I knew I couldn't get a fellowship," I did not want to promote the fellowships and have to disappoint a lot of the applicants.

I began calling the major contributors to the endowment to ask, "Should we dip into the principal to award a significant number of fellowships or should we just not award any this year?" NEH said that no one would look at how we had spent our money unless we later applied for another grant; McCune and Hearst said we could do whatever we thought best. When I was speaking to Bill Bowen, the chief financial officer from Berea College, Lee Jones, came into my office and overheard our conversation. Lee pointed out that, at that time, it was illegal in KY for a non-profit to invade the principal; when Bowen heard that, he said, "Why don't we send you an emergency grant of $150,000 for

---

70. The contribution that I remember most came from a fellowship recipient at a small college in NC. It was a check for $1,000. I called him and said, "I know what you make; I never expected you to make such a generous donation." He replied, "I made $10,000 in royalties on the book I wrote during my fellowship, and I thought I should give the ACA at least ten percent of it."

awards this year." With that and the $100,000 of interest the ACA had earned, we could offer a respectable number of awards.

Even with the generosity of Mellon and others, we still could give significantly fewer fellowships than we had been awarding. For example, in 1996 thirty-two faculty from twenty-three colleges received a total of $646,500 in fellowship awards. In 1997-1998, the ACA awarded forty-seven fellowships; $728,575 was the total amount awarded, with $464,050 from Mellon and $264,525 from an anonymous foundation. By 2000, when we were dependent on the endowment income, only twenty fellowships (roughly half the previous number) were awarded to faculty from thirteen of the ACA colleges. Despite funds being added to the endowment as new contributions came in, the endowment income was only $358,271. Our financial advisors claimed the low return was the result of global disturbances leading to the major collapse in the market several years later. But we never heard complaints about how few fellowships were being awarded because we had so many other opportunities that were grant funded and not dependent on earnings from the endowment, such as international study experiences, faculty workshops, faculty-student research grants, and experiences with arts organizations in Pittsburgh.

For example, in 2002, when only seventeen fellowships (from thirteen colleges) were awarded, eighty faculty had travel grants; twenty faculty with forty-five students studied abroad; 336 attended the annual Summit; twenty-six faculty attended the workshop in Pittsburgh on how to incorporate the teaching of opera into various courses, such as physics; forty-two women attended a conference on Women in Administration; and thirty-four faculty participated in the Writing-Across-the-Curriculum workshops—with all or most expenses covered by ACA grants. Carol Boggess, a faculty member who received grant support to write the definitive biography of James Still, sent a note to the ACA about the impact of the ACA opportunities on those at Mars Hill College: a travel grant supported a faculty presentation at a major conference; a fellowship supported a sabbatical that jump-started a publishing career; shared access to the Foundation Directory Online helped a new grant writer; another faculty member's teaching and scholarship were enhanced by an ACA trip to Turkey; another faculty member received support to travel to China to prepare for teaching a course in "Confucianism, Taoism, and Zen." And almost every other ACA college could have reported similar benefits.[71]

The graduate deans on the Fellowship Review Committee frequently talked about how impressed they were with the ACA fellowship recipients who had residency at their universities. One professor called the graduate dean at his university and said that he had never had a student as bright as the one he was working with from the ACA program. And it was not just the intelligence and dedication to their work that impressed those from outside the ACA influence. A sense of humility and lack of selfishness was typical of the fellows. Once a fellowship recipient emailed me to say that when I was visiting his campus, he wanted to meet with me. When we met, he said that he had written in his proposal for the ACA fellowship that he would finish three chapters of his dissertation during the summer of the award, but he had only finished two chapters. He thought he should give back one-third of the money he had received.

---

71. See Appendix B for a listing of awards made from 1993-2008 (based on annual reports published for those years). I didn't receive copies of those reports until this memoir was completed so the information from them was not incorporated into the main body of this document.

I explained to him how few people actually accomplish what they think they will in the time they anticipate, and, while the ACA expected him to let us know when he finished the dissertation, he did not need to return any money.

Endowing Opportunities for Students

Another major contribution to the ACA endowment came from a source that contacted us to ask if we could help fulfill their mission. Colonel Lee B. Ledford had grown up in Harlan, KY. According to *Wikipedia*, the population there in 2010 was 1,745; the population had dropped every decade since 1950 when it was 4,786. The per capita income was $15,572. The name "Bloody Harlan" came from a strike of coal miners in the early 1970s that lasted over a year. In short, Colonel Ledford grew up in a poor county with a reputation for violence. Still, he excelled in school, ended up at West Point, and made a career of military service before retiring to practice law on Wall Street.

Having no children or other relatives he felt close to, when his health began failing, Colonel Ledford moved to Carmel, about an hour from Manhattan, and hired a caretaker. As he began thinking about his legacy and the significant wealth he had acquired, he developed a living trust that would provide support to help students in eastern KY pursue a path similar to his. He did not want money used to administer the awards, so his lawyer gave him a list of non-profit colleges and other agencies that could administer a program with his money for the purpose he described—without administrative overhead. I do not know how many agencies or schools were on that list, but I understand that Morehead State University was second on it, and the ACA was first. Funding from the Trust was designated for a foundation that would give ninety percent of the income to an organization that could help students from eastern KY get a good college education; ten percent was to go to West Point.

Some information about about the foundation and the trust can be found at https://caselaw.findlaw.com/ny-supreme-court/1416038.html. This link is to the lawsuit involving Claude Hill, a long-time friend of Colonel Ledford who lived in Bristol, VA, but visited the Colonel in New York frequently, and Frank Bolden, the caretaker. The lawsuit revolved around whether Bolden was entitled to all the property he had claimed. Copies of the relevant information about the multiple lawsuits related to the property of Colonel Ledford, some presented in the Surrogate Court and others in the Supreme Court of Putnam County in New York State, are stored at the ACA office in Bristol, TN, and in archives at Berea College.

Colonel Ledford's lawyer called to tell me that a major part of the estate would be used to establish a foundation and asked if the ACA could fulfill the Colonel's wish for his money. My response was, "I didn't know someone could set up a foundation and name the beneficiary to receive the money." The lawyer explained that many foundations designate beneficiaries, and he asked me to send him the papers verifying the ACA's tax-exempt status, and he would establish the Ledford Foundation. I explained that the ACA did not work with public schools to encourage students to go to college, and if we started a program to do that, we would have to charge for the administration of it. I added that the ACA does provide funding for students at the member colleges to conduct research with faculty or to do some independent project overseen by faculty. Participating in an ACA summer project provides income to the student so he or she does not have to work at Walmart or McDonald's during the summer. With Ledford money, we could increase those awards to encourage students to stay in college and finish their degrees.

Some months later, I had a call about a meeting on a Thursday (in 2000), but Colonel Ledford died several days before the scheduled meeting and it was cancelled. A month or more later, I called the lawyer to ask if the foundation had been developed; he said that it had been, but he could not tell me anything else because he had been fired. He told me to call Michael Quis, the accountant the Colonel had contacted after receiving a flyer promoting Quis' services. When I called and asked about plans to meet, I learned the date of the upcoming meeting but was told I did not need to come because it was just an organizational meeting. I insisted that I wanted to come. There was a long pause; then I heard, "The meeting is at 9:00 a.m.—I mean 10:00."

I flew to New York, took a train to Carmel, and took a taxi to Quis' office at the back of his house. When I stepped through the door, I was at the bottom of stairs that led up to a small meeting room. It was clear that the meeting had started. I heard one person say, "Shouldn't we wait for the lady from Kentucky to get here?" I decided that even though I was early for a 10:00 a.m. meeting, I was late for one that started at 9:00, and I took the stairs and found a group of five men squeezed around a small table: Quis, Frank Bolden (Colonel Ledford's caretaker), Claude Hill (Ledford's friend from Bristol, TN), Brian O'Connor (Ledford's long-time friend and financial advisor),[72] and

---

72. On my way out of the meeting, O'Connor followed me, asking if he could manage the Ledford money that the ACA would eventually receive. I never responded to his request, and a short time after the meeting, I learned that O'Connor had been convicted of a federal crime, would soon go to jail, and wanted to name his replacement to be on the board of the Ledford Foundation while he was in prison.

one other person whose name or relationships to Colonel Ledford I do not remember. The lawyer who had been fired came for a short time to answer questions. He could barely squeeze into the room to sit in the only chair in a corner of the room away from the table.

When I asked how much money the ACA would receive that year, Quis said, "We won't give money this year." The lawyer pointed out that no money had been awarded for almost two years, and the executors were legally obligated to give some that year. Shortly after the meeting, the ACA received a check for $75,000.

After the lawyer left the meeting, one of the men said that he wanted me to give some of the money the ACA would receive to a culinary school in New York, where his son attended. Another said he thought the Putnam County Sheriff's Office should receive a contribution because they were so much help during the Colonel's last years—in transporting him to and from the hospital. I said that the ACA could not fund people or organizations outside the central Appalachian region. Near noon, someone asked when I needed to get back to the train station. I replied that there were trains going back to the city every couple of hours after lunch. Then Quis stood up and said that his secretary would take me back to the train station so I could get back to New York in time for lunch.

I arrived back in Manhattan by 2:00 p.m. and went straight to the office of the Mellon Foundation. I met with Tish Emerson and said, "I've met a lot of scoundrels in my day, but I've never met five at one time." As Bill Bowen walked by the door to her office, Tish stopped him and asked me to tell the story of my day in Carmel. Bowen said he had a friend who was a retired lawyer and had signed a noncompete agreement so he could not represent me in court, but, informally, he could give me advice; that friend became my pro bono advisor for roughly a year. His primary advice was to stay out of the fray as much as possible.

As the dispute continued, in 2001 we selected thirty-two Ledford Scholars from eleven ACA colleges with the $75,000 we had received. I stayed in touch with Bowen's lawyer friend but did not even try to keep up with what was happening related to the Ledford Foundation; then I had a call from the lawyer and learned that "there is too much smoke; there is going to be a court case," and I needed a lawyer who could represent me in court. Then he assured me the ACA would be fine because the case would eventually end up in Attorney General Elliot Spitzer's office, and he would settle everything. His confidence in Spitzer was a bit misplaced; as someone told me when I complained that Spitzer's office had been of little help, "You don't vote in New York." I even had a friend in the office of the attorney general in KY call Spitzer's office to assure him the ACA was a legitimate organization. My friend called me back and said, "Spitzer's people couldn't love you more," but there was no indication of how he was going to "settle" anything.

Bowen's friend who had been advising me informally recommended Fred Sembler to represent the ACA.[73] Sembler had just left a large law firm that had been involved in the lawsuit regarding Doris Duke (whose caretaker had gone to court over her estate); and he was setting up his own law practice so, the lawyer assured me, his fees would not be as high as most New York lawyers charged. As I was leaving my first visit with Sembler, he said that he "had never felt more on

---

73. The contracts said he was representing me, which meant, I was assured, he was representing the ACA. I would have felt better if the name of the chairperson of the ACA board had also been listed on the court documents.

the side of the angels." I did not anticipate that, with the angels on our side, the case would take almost four years to settle.

I confess that I never attended any of the court cases, and Sembler had told me not to talk to any of the parties involved or to their lawyers, but to refer all contacts to him. I never paid much attention to what was happening as the court cases advanced. At some point the benefits Bolden, the Colonel's caretaker, was entitled to were determined. There was no denying that Bolden had served the Colonel well for many years and that the Colonel had given Bolden his power of attorney in 1997. When the case was settled, Bolden received multiple benefits, but he had to relinquish many other resources because he had transferred them to himself after Colonel Ledford had died. From my perspective, this lawsuit would make a great case history for some scholar of the law. I have insisted that the ACA office keep all the documents the courts were ready to destroy; when the boxes increased beyond what the ACA staff thought was more than they could store, the president at Berea College accepted the extra record boxes to be stored in the archives of the college.

I could not keep up with which court was deciding what issue. The case got more and more complicated, with two different judges for the two courts involved (Surrogate and Supreme). Each of the parties involved in the case had a lawyer, and the Association of Graduates of the US Military Academy came to the table claiming that their organization deserved a higher percentage of the gains from the endowment than ten percent.

I could not understand why West Point needed money. Someone explained to me that the federal government does cover expenses for students at West Point, but there are a number of private (i.e., expensive) preparatory schools that help students meet the requirements for West Point; Ledford's money was to be used to send promising students to those schools. The Association of Graduates of West Point insisted that their documents indicated the strong interest the Colonel had in helping students from eastern KY get a good secondary school education and go to West Point.

At one point the representative from West Point wanted me to apologize for taking $75,000 of the money from the Colonel's estate before it was determined the ACA was entitled to it. Since I never saw any of the courtroom drama, I did not learn of this demand for an apology until long after the case was settled. The ACA board members finally agreed that West Point could have twenty-five percent, not just the ten percent specified by the relevant documents. They could not argue with the point made by West Point that the Colonel knew their organization better than he knew the ACA.

I learned that part of our settlement would be rental property in Lancaster, KY, about twenty minutes from Berea, that Ledford had owned. The property was four duplexes. The ACA presidents insisted that I sell all the property when I mentioned that the ACA could keep the rental property and use the income to increase benefits for future Ledford Scholars. The person managing the rentals for the Colonel put a notice in newspapers in Garrard and surrounding counties, indicating when he would be available to show the property and the closing date for all sealed bids. When the closing date arrived, I opened the bids which had arrived close to the deadline; no bid was anywhere near the appraised value. We developed a plan which would include selling some of the duplexes to one bidder and others to a different bidder. Then, I postponed contacting the people who had made the bids and pulled out the file folder for the property to put away the various offers. Inside the folder was a sealed envelope; it had been received shortly after the property had first been advertised, and it was a bid for the appraised value of all the property.

In the summer of 2001, I flew to New York to meet with Assistant Attorney General William Josephson, in charge of charities under Elliot Spitzer. That first meeting was supposed to include the parties on the other side of the case, but they never appeared. Since part of the meeting was to determine how much the Association of Graduates of the US Military Academy would agree to as a settlement, the West Point lawyer was also supposed to be present, but he did not attend. I was, once again, in a state of shock: how could the attorney general call a meeting and have everyone except my lawyer and me ignore him? After Sembler and I left Josephson's office, I called the head of the West Point Association and asked if I could come to meet with him to talk about the settlement; he was very gracious and set up a time we could meet the next day; then several hours later, his office called to tell me the lawyer handling West Point's position in the case said there was no need for me to come to talk about the case; the West Point lawyers were handling it.

Josephson rescheduled our meeting for 9 a.m. on September 11. I flew into New York, checked into the Edison Hotel (between Broadway and 7th Ave, near Time Square) and met with Sembler on Monday, September 10. The next morning, I got into a cab going down Broadway; passing St. Vincent's Hospital, I noticed lots of gurneys and hospital personnel on the side of the street and ambulances speeding toward the World Trade Center where the Twin Towers had been attacked.[74] At the foot of Broadway, where Canal Street crosses, there were crowds of people running toward Canal Street; the cab driver told me I had to get out there, that he couldn't get through the crowd to reach the office of the attorney general at 120 Broadway. I said, "I'm not getting out to go that way; all those people are coming this way."

I rolled down my window to ask one of the people running by the cab what was happening. She said, "We're being invaded" and reached into the cab to unlock the door and slide in beside me. She said she didn't care where I was going, she was going there too. But when I asked where she wanted to go, she said, "To my brother's office in the heart of Manhattan." I had the driver drop me at Sembler's office where I was able to use his land line to call the ACA office and let people know I was not in the World Trade Center. Cell phones seemed not to be working anywhere in the city.[75]

Most of the hotels in the area immediately closed to anyone who did not have a key for a room there. The Edison was a bit slow to close so I was able to walk back in and ask for an extension to my stay. I had already checked out of the hotel, and the desk clerk told me the hotel was full for the night. A nice older couple in line behind me said that I could share their room if I needed a place to stay. Then the manager of the hotel came out and gave me the key to the room I had left.

---

74. Much of the preparation of the hospital personnel proved futile; most of those injured had died before any rescue could take place.

75. My assistant said my daughter and a couple of my friends had called to check on me. I asked, "Has my husband called?" Her response was, "You know him; he is probably in a classroom teaching Shakespeare and doesn't know that the world is coming to an end." Later, he explained he had called the hotel where I was staying and they said I was still checked in. It never occurred to him that if I were dead in the rubble of the Twin Towers, I could still be registered at the hotel.

Although every room was booked, since the airport was closed, there were sure to be cancellations. When I reached my room, Mr. Josephson was calling to say that since we couldn't meet that morning and since I would be stuck in New York the next day, he wanted Sembler and me to come to his house in Brooklyn the next afternoon to talk about the Ledford Foundation.

I was supposed to meet with Mellon that afternoon; I called the Foundation and was told I should come to their office and stay for dinner. There was no indication which restaurants would be open, so they had ordered food to be brought to their office. Since they had not mentioned lunch, I stopped on my way to their office and ate lunch—only to learn when I arrived at the Mellon office that they had held lunch for me and were expecting me for dinner. That was one of many times when I ate two lunches rather than offend a potential donor.

We watched the tragedies unfolding at the World Trade Center all afternoon, and after dinner, as I was walking the deserted streets of Manhattan to return to my hotel, a cab pulled over; in the back seat were two men in scrubs. The taxi driver said that he was not supposed to be transporting anybody but medical personnel, but I looked like I was going their way. So, I had a ride for the ten or so blocks back to the Hotel Edison.

The next morning, I called Ilene Mack at the Hearst Foundation and asked if I could come for a visit; she said that would be great. But by the time I got to her office, people there had realized they knew someone who had been killed; it became obvious that no one there was interested in talking about the ACA.

That afternoon, as Sembler and I were taking a subway to Brooklyn, the subway stopped, and an announcement was made that we would arrive in Brooklyn but then the subway would be closed because the vibrations it was causing were making more of the Twin Towers collapse. No one on that subway but me seemed concerned enough to stop reading their papers or books. Sembler and I arrived at Josephson's townhouse late in the afternoon and sat with him on a small back porch, overlooking a small backyard, surrounded by tall brick buildings. I went through the history of the ACA and Sembler talked a little about the case. At one point, I said, "I have worked with lots of foundations—Mellon, Pew, Exxon, Hearst, etc.—but I have never encountered any like the Ledford Foundation. Josephson asked, "What do you think makes the Ledford Foundation different?" My response was, "Greed."

After we left Josephson's, Sembler told me we needed to walk a couple of blocks to get to a working subway back to Manhattan. My response was, "Please, don't put me on another subway." I asked about taking a cab; he said I should look around; there were no cabs running. Then he said we could walk to his apartment and get his car and he would drive me back. As we were walking, we passed a car service office that was open. When we went in and asked if someone could drive me back to Manhattan, the response was, "We'll have to charge a lot for that trip tonight." I asked, "How much is 'a lot?'" "Fifty dollars." Sembler said, "I'll take you." I said, "No, you charge two hundred dollars an hour." The car service driver did not seem concerned about the situation in the city, but as we were about to cross the Brooklyn Bridge back to Manhattan, the car was searched. It had been a memorable two days.

By Thursday, September 13, I was ready to leave NY. As I was checking out of the hotel for the second time, the manager came to the desk to tell me that I just needed to call if I changed my mind about leaving the city, that there would be a room if I wanted to come back.

I thought perhaps I could get a bus to take me back to KY, but the bus station was closed. A police officer on duty at the corner near the bus station suggested I take a train to Philadelphia and get a flight from there to KY. He cautioned me not to stand in any lines; just to get a ticket from a kiosk. A few minutes later I was on a train to Philadelphia. At the train station in Philadelphia, another passenger on the train shared a cab with me to the Philadelphia Airport. There were almost no passengers, but all the airlines had agents available. I asked about flights. One agent told me that their planes were supposed to be flying but none had left yet that day; then she said that there was a flight coming from Louisville, KY, and as soon as it arrived, the plane would return to Louisville. I had dinner, the plane arrived, and the two other passengers and I flew first class to Louisville. The flight attendant suggested I get a car service to drive me to Lexington (about ninety minutes away) since, she said, taxi drivers cannot negotiate prices the way the drivers for car services can. By the time I reached home that night, I could say I had experienced a memorable four days.

While Sembler's charges were probably much less than those most other lawyers would have charged, when we had paid him about $220,000, I declared the ACA could not afford to continue to claim a right to the Colonel's money. By this point, with the other parties perhaps paying their lawyers out of Ledford's Living Trust, I had no idea how much money might be left; I had never even been given a figure for the amount available at the death of the Colonel. Ed Welch, chair of the ACA Governing Board at the time, had a different perspective. At the June meeting of the presidents, he gave an impassioned plea with the final statement, "We can't let the turkeys win!" Each president increased the dues for membership in the ACA by four dollars per FTE for the next year to help cover the cost of continuing the fight. When Bowen learned of our plight, including the possibility that the lawsuit could continue for another year or two, he called Barbara Paul Robinson.

In addition to being the first woman to serve as president of the New York City Bar in its history of one hundred twenty-five years, Barbara was a partner at Debevoise and Plimpton, one of the best-known of international law firms; she was the first woman partner in the firm and had served as head of the Trusts and Estates Department there. Apparently, she didn't hesitate when Bowen called and asked her to serve the ACA on a pro bono basis. With her agreement, I went to Sembler's office to explain to him that while we had not been dissatisfied with his services, we could not turn down the offer of a major lawyer in a major New York law firm to represent the ACA from this point forward on a pro bono basis.

Within a few months, Barbara had settled the case. The Ledford Foundation was dissolved, the ACA received seventy-five percent of the money available, and West Point Association of Graduates received twenty-five percent. Each association was to create an endowment to support the projects Colonel Ledford had wanted to encourage.

I have only a vague picture of Barbara's approach in the Putnam County Court Room. I heard that she began by saying that she was now the lawyer representing the ACA; she was not charging the ACA for the time of her law office or for any expenses, so there was no way the other parties would "wear the ACA down." Later she explained that her office had determined that Hill and Quis and others involved had failed to fulfill their legal obligations as trustees of the Ledford Foundation and were personally liable for back taxes as well as for the penalties and interest, but she would not pursue that case if they ended their fight to deny the

ACA money that the Colonel clearly intended for the non-profit to have. The final amount the ACA received, including the sale of the duplexes, was about $3.7 million. I tried not to think of how much money we might have received if there had not been a four-year lawsuit.

A May 23, 2003, note to me indicated that Barbara had held the West Point Association of Graduates to the condition that if they received twenty-five percent of the Ledford estate, the money had to be limited to supporting Appalachian students from Harlan and other Central Appalachian counties or the money not awarded would go back to the ACA. It might be interesting to check to see that West Point has fulfilled that obligation.

Figures reflecting funding from the ACA for Ledford awards indicate that in 2004, ten students from six colleges received $25,500; in 2005, thirty-eight students from twelve colleges were awarded $132,112; in 2006, forty-one from sixteen schools received $190,229; in 2007, thirty-seven from thirteen colleges received funding (but I don't have the total amount awarded). In 2008, forty-nine students from thirteen colleges were awarded $101,338. The settlement was finalized in the summer of 2003, and on a weekend after the settlement, when many of the ACA presidents were in New York for other purposes, the ACA hosted a dinner in Barbara's honor and gave her a collection of books by Appalachian writers, many signed by the authors.

An opportunity for students from ACA colleges that resulted from the lawsuit, in addition to the Ledford Scholarships for research, is the Robinson Scholarships for Law School, now funded by Barbara Paul Robinson herself. These scholarships originated to support graduates from ACA colleges who have been accepted into law school and intend to practice law in Appalachia. The scholarships were initially funded from the Alf Canon Fund, money remaining from the time the ACA was based at Warren Wilson College, to show our appreciation to Barbara. Later, Barbara herself continued to fund students with awards of $2,500 for each of two years. Barbara has supported past recipients of these fellowships by taking several to New York to observe the practice of law in a large city. Her advice on an informal basis before and after my retirement has continued to be invaluable to me.

Library Resources and Technology

For the next two major initiatives of the ACA, I have to defer to those who led those initiatives. Since both of these programs required knowing or learning new technologies, I never fully understood the work in which the ACA staff and many faculty and students from the member colleges participated. As I said to Tish when she complained that the grant I had written to Mellon for support related to technology did not say anything except that if Mellon gave me a million dollars I would do something and it would have something to do with technology: "That is all I can promise." What convinced Mellon to give me four million dollars after that first one million for technology was the people I hired to oversee the ACA work with technology.

The Central Library, which started when JSTOR was introduced to the public, preceded most of our work with technology and increased interest in the services information technology could provide. Services and resources of the Central Library were quickly incorporated into the libraries at the then thirty-seven colleges, in part because there were strong librarians at most of the colleges who had worked for those colleges for a long time, and it was clear from the beginning of the ACA work with libraries that the colleges could save money and increase resources almost immediately. Trying to centralize computer technologies for all the member colleges was more complicated, especially given the poor connectivity at many of those colleges and the few staff available for instruction related to technology. When the University of Richmond in VA had about nineteen tech support staff members, most ACA colleges had one or none. But I am trying to write about something I have little knowledge or understanding of; those who led the Central Library and the technology programs for the ACA can better explain them.

William G. Bowen Central Library of Appalachia

What became perhaps the most important opportunity offered by the ACA, at least in terms of what the presidents seemed to value, was a Central Library developed for the ACA by Tony Krug. When he started helping the ACA, Tony was head librarian at Bethany College in WV. Following is the information Tony sent to report his reflections about the developments that led to what is now the William G. Bowen Central Library of Appalachia:

As I recall, you sent an open letter out to all ACA library directors during the Christmas season 1995 or '96 about Mellon's plans for JSTOR[76] and how that might relate to ACA libraries. I responded as

---

76. JSTOR provides online access to more than twelve million academic journal articles, books, and primary sources in seventy-five disciplines.

did one other librarian, Cy Dillon, at Ferrum. Many libraries were closed during the holidays, but that is when Mellon asked you for a response - you told me later. Anyway, Cy did not think JSTOR would help, while I praised the concept of JSTOR. However, it was noted the initial upfront fee of $10,000 was totally out of the question for Bethany's library, and I suspected for most other ACA libraries, no matter how splendid the concept and benefit. Based on those initial reactions, you and Tish decided I was your man to help with a Mellon grant to the ACA to cover those initial fees and an endowment to underwrite a percentage of the annual subscription fee to make JSTOR affordable for ACA libraries.

I must point out that my work was done in close relationship with a team of ACA library directors, as well as with you and Tish. And, although he had doubts originally, Cy Dillon was a leader among our ACA libraries, as well as in Virginia libraries. He was an officer in the Virginia Library Association when this article was published in 2004: https://ejournals.lib.vt.edu/valib/article/view/939/1220.

The initial JSTOR grant was to bring only twenty-two libraries in. Some of the libraries were on campuses that did not have internet at all or had internet only for administrative functions. Meetings were held with library directors to discuss how the funds would be dispersed. JSTOR was seen as highly desirable to nearly all librarians, although training would be needed, since even the libraries that did have internet capability did not have anything like JSTOR. As librarians talked to their administrators about JSTOR many campuses determined they would not want to be left out. The whole project raised the need for internet connections in the libraries to a much higher level of campus concern. This is particularly noteworthy on those campuses where this type of consideration was not a concern at all previously.

Given the interest stirred, Mellon was gracious enough to expand funding to all libraries and to initiate funding for library administration and library teaching conferences, then to encourage the development of online collections through the cooperative purchasing of other resources to complement the JSTOR centerpiece of online collections. As JSTOR capabilities developed, integration with online catalogs for example, it became clear that ACA libraries did not all have online catalogs and those that did had an array of systems that would not easily allow for maximum use of JSTOR. So, Mellon helped launch a shared catalog concept that was developed along the shared costs idea that the shared online collections initiated. By sharing overhead costs, libraries could have a higher quality catalog at the same or lower cost of the catalog in place, if there was a catalog in place. For various reasons, not all of the ACA libraries chose to participate in the shared catalog, but participation quickly grew to eighty percent or more and has stayed at about that level of participation despite some fluctuation in ACA membership and catalog participation.

The library activity of the ACA was found to be attractive to some colleges without ACA membership, which led to membership expansion in North Carolina and Tennessee. Although the ACA has suffered the loss of a couple of institutions there still is a net gain in membership for the ACA overall from the impact of the library work.

For individual campuses, the ACA Central Library brought electronic, digital, online academic scholarship to a much higher level, in some cases where it never had existed at all previously as a part of the academic processes. Of particular note are the campus-based faculty workshops the libraries sponsored for campus faculty to learn to use the new materials available. Along those lines, the introduction of Artstor[77] was an attempt to not only provide a digital assist to scholarship, but also to add a multimedia flair. The libraries in the ACA, and the conduct of academic work on their campuses, has been forever changed by the impact of the ACA library projects.

ACA campus libraries often were, and are, storekeepers of the heritage of their campuses, and even the organizations that developed the campus. ACA library archives joined together to form the Digital Library of Appalachia that contributes significantly to a better understanding of the campuses and the region.

What came to be known as the Bowen Central Library of Appalachia is the umbrella for five major efforts that continue to bear fruit now, over twenty years since its inception:

1. The unification, organization, and improved professional image of the library staffs of the individual ACA libraries in programs that continue to foster and promote librarianship in the new practices of an "information age" for all member libraries.

2. The shared collections the libraries purchased and maintain jointly, beginning with JSTOR and Artstor, and expanded to many additional electronic journals and books for all thirty-five member libraries.

3. The ACA Shared Catalog, currently serving twenty-eight libraries with a top-end online catalog that fully serves the extensive online, as well as the local physical holdings of each library.

---

77. The Artstor Digital Library features a wide range of multidisciplinary content from some of the world's top museums, artists, libraries, scholars, and photo archives, including rare collections not accessible anywhere else.

4. *The Digital Library of Appalachia which offers unique archival digital images, recordings, and printed materials from twenty-three ACA colleges.*

5. *The library staff development programs dovetailed with an ACA library program distributed governance system to meaningfully involve personnel in all phases of library services across all campuses. Staff development was an area of support for the other four parts of the Bowen Central Library. What was especially significant with staff development was the community spirit that crossed campus rivalries, internal friction in the different areas of library work, and the different administrative styles of the various campus and library administrations. At times, the librarians involved marveled at how smoothly the ACA library programs functioned and grew.*

It is hard for me to convey how valuable Dr. Krug's leadership was in the development of the Central Library. As he explained in the article referenced above:

In 2003, the ACA Central Library reported a total of $40.5 million in benefits. Each of the thirty-four colleges in counties designated as Appalachian ... received more than $1 million in benefits in return for dues of $12.18 per FTE (Full Time Equivalent Student). This represents a return on investment averaging approximately $75 per dues dollar invested. In addition, group purchasing, distributed according to individual campus needs beyond the core/universal collections and services provided for all, brought returns in excess of ten dollars per dollar expended. The impact of the ACA Central Library varies from campus to campus, with campuses as small as 500 students to as large as 3,500 students representing over a dozen diverse denominations and philosophical commitments in their founding. Total FTE for the thirty-four colleges in 2003 was 37,000.

It is easy to understand how valuable the core digital collections, cooperative licensing system for the shared library system, and professional development opportunities for librarians would be to a small library with extremely limited financial resources. It took me a long time to believe the presidents were unhappy in any way with the director of the new William G. Bowen Central Library of Appalachia.

The first indication that the presidents of the member colleges were not as happy as the librarians with the development of the Central Library came when one of the presidents spoke at an annual meeting: "Alice, you think like my wife: she buys a two-hundred-dollar dress on sale for one hundred dollars, tells me how she saved one hundred dollars, and then lets the dress hang in her closet unworn." My response was that it seemed to me that being able to say that students at an ACA college have access to the same library resources as students at major universities would help increase enrollments. "Your wife doesn't know when she might need that dress." That argument was not one that was convincing to that president, but he was kind enough not to bring it up again.

Soon after engaging in this dress-online resources analogy, I learned that the president of Berea was about to take Berea College off the list of participating libraries. Shortly afterwards, I met one of Berea's trustees at the Louisville airport. When I asked him what the ACA offered that was most valuable to Berea College, his response was, "The Central Library." My confusion was alleviated when I learned that the head of Berea's library had prepared a chart for the president indicating the savings Berea was acquiring by being part of the Central Library. Cost savings had always been the benefit that most attracted the presidents to the ACA. While fellowships and travel grants to faculty were something most considered "nice," some of the deans and presidents feared that such professional development opportunities only benefited the faculty participants. Having a ledger that showed how the economies of scale provided by the ACA reduced the costs of necessary resources brought more attention to the ACA. I should have known that cost savings would be the factor that would convince the presidents to approve an ACA benefit. The first time they had paid much attention to the FSP at UK was when AT&T provided a warehouse full of computers for distribution to some of the colleges.

Tony was already addressing concerns by the time I learned about them. He had indicated that each campus needed to host workshops to help faculty understand the new library technology so they could use it wisely. With funding from Mellon, there were projects called Faculty Enrichment in Library Technology (FELT) and Library Experiences with Technology and Training (LETT).

Benefits of the Library continued to increase. At the end of 1999, benefits at each college ranged from $1,200 to $12,000. Tony continued to impress the program officers at Mellon, pointing out that the Central Library needed to consider the issue of sustainability. When the goals of the six-year grant awarded in 1997 were exceeded by the end of 1999, Tony asked for and the Mellon Foundation allowed the money remaining for that project to be considered a quasi-endowment to support on-going activities of the various committees that had been established for the Library, as well as to address the need for more administrative staff to assist with the Central Library.

Then the presidents began to complain about the quasi-endowment, questioning why a staff member of the ACA should have so much control of an ACA account. They seemed to think that Tony was working toward making the Library an entity independent of the ACA—and them. I never thought that Tony wanted to leave the ACA; we were certainly good to him. He was the only staff member who had an ACA car, although the car he selected was small and energy efficient despite the fact that he was a large man. He made his own schedule and that of his assistants. He was the only ACA staff person whom I asked to recommend his own salary, based on the grants he had received and expenses he anticipated. For most of the ACA staff, I had written the grants they were administering, and I had a clear sense of how much their salaries should be. Also, I had established Tony's salary when he first began working with the ACA and until I realized that he had a strong sense of integrity and would not recommend a salary for himself that would have been hard to justify.

Then Tony wrote a new proposal that included a comprehensive plan to assure the future of the Central Library when funding might not be available from outside agencies such as foundations and federal agencies. A core collection of electronic books, serials, media, and reference works and increased Central Library services was developed, as was a funding structure that involved grant funds as well as matching dollars from the member colleges to sustain the ACA library. In Tony's mind, as the Library was providing collections and services centrally, spending at campus libraries could be reduced, allowing saved dollars to be redirected to specific needs at each campus library and contributions to sustain the ACA Central Library. The presidents grew more concerned with every mention Tony made about "contributions to the ACA" by the participating libraries. While most of the presidents were happy to see cost savings for library expenditures, few expected those savings to be made available for their librarians to pay more to sustain and expand the Central Library. Tony and the presidents were growing further and further apart in their expectations.

When the presidents expressed concern about how much money Tony could access, how quickly their librarians responded to his requests, and how Tony did not seem to answer the questions presidents asked as fully as they wanted, it never occurred to me that they would one day tell me to fire him. What I did know was that Tony had become critical to the colleges utilizing the Central Library and the fact that he did not seem to answer to me (or to the presidents) did not bother me since he (1) was always respectful, (2) turned in his annual reports on time for my review before sending them to Mellon, and (3) continued to collect multiple vocal and written notices of praise from the campus librarians and the agencies supporting the work of the Central Library.

I understood so little about online library resources that I depended on Tony to find funding. For example, when Tony began to organize a Digital Library of Appalachia, he received federal funding for the individual libraries to digitize the collections they held that were related to the history of the region. Tony had discovered that there were many highly valuable collections on ACA college campuses, but few were housed in facilities that would protect them for future access. For example, one college had some valuable documents stored in the crawl space under a campus building.

I was reassured that Tony's job was secure when I heard stories about librarians at the member colleges who turned down better-paying jobs saying, "Where else could I get to do what I can, and get the support I have, than in the ACA?" One librarian commented that she currently knew more about the professional work of a librarian two states away than she had known about her own staff ten years before.[78] She had grown in her field as a result of this new perspective. Another librarian wrote that she now had more electronic books available than hard copies. With all the new opportunities and resources available and the praise of the librarians, I never made it clear to Tony that he needed to be more responsive to the concerns of the presidents.

I have to admit that I always paid more attention to advice from foundations and other sources funding ACA projects than I did to the ACA presidents. I believed that if those agencies lost interest in the ACA, the ACA would not survive.[79] Tony paid attention to those at the Mellon Foundation, from which most of the funding for the Central Library came, and to the program officers at NEH. He also listened to the librarians at ACA colleges and was dedicated to helping them build the kind of digital libraries that could compare favorably with those at elite private colleges and those at research universities.

I knew Mellon was pleased with the development and progress of the Central Library and the Digital Library. Mellon staff had used one of Tony's annual reports to the foundation as an example of how a report should be written; when Mellon had indicated Tony needed to be full-time, and Tony said he could not work full time on a grant that could end at any time—that he needed a more secure income—Bowen's response was, "Endow his position." And Mellon gave the ACA the money to endow Tony's salary. In recognition of the support of

---

78. I was pleased by this comment especially because what I wanted to see was faculty (and librarians) looking outside their immediate community for new ideas and using that information to impact their colleges.

79. This was before the endowment was established.

the foundation under Bill Bowen's leadership, we named the library the William G. Bowen Central Library of Appalachia (BCLA). When the chair of the ACA Governing Board asked if I were afraid to fire Tony, my response was, "No, I'm afraid to make Mellon mad." So long as Mellon, NEH, and the librarians at the member colleges were happy with the work of the Central Library, I thought all was well. I should have been paying more attention to a program that I thought didn't need my attention.

Clearly, I was paying too much attention to the views of authorities outside the ACA and not enough to the concerns of the ACA presidents. When Eugene, my secretary at UK, moved to Berea to work with me at the new ACA office, her comment after our first meeting with the ACA Executive Committee was, "That was a good meeting, but you were strange." "How was I strange?" Her answer was that I didn't argue with anybody; I didn't even talk very much. My response was, "Yes, that's the problem with working with college presidents; you have to at least pretend you have respect for their authority." But after over ten years at the ACA, I was growing less inclined to pretend.

One of the presidents heard me talking to Larry Shinn, at that time president of Berea College.

"You can't talk to him like that," the person overhearing the conversation said.

"Why can't I?"

"He's your board."

"No, he's not." I replied. "He is 1/35th of my board, and surely the rest of you don't agree with him."

By the time I was being told to fire the head of the Bowen Central Library of Appalachia, I had ceased to remember my own advice, and I wasn't even pretending to respect the authority of the presidents.[80] But as the presidents became more vocal about Tony's shortcomings according to their expectations and when Tish Emerson came to the ACA office to do an evaluation of the ACA, and she heard about the struggle between Tony and the presidents and the silo created for the Central Library, and I realized I was only about a year from retiring, I knew whoever took my place would certainly follow the order of the presidents at least for a year or so. I told Tony he needed to leave the Central Library and asked if he wanted to resign or retire. I did know that all those librarians who loved working with Tony would not be fooled by my use of those words; they would know I had fired him and not understand why. They held a farewell event for Tony and showered him with gifts. He accepted a position at one of the ACA colleges in TN, close to his home, and I was left to find someone to lead the Central Library with the vision and energy Tony had exemplified.

A friend who read a draft of this memoir asked me if I ever came to have sympathy with the position of the presidents who thought Tony should be fired. I don't remember ever once thinking that the presidents were right to have their concerns about Tony's independent spirit; I do remember being surprised that one of the retired academic deans who had worked for several months in the ACA office strongly supported the position of the presidents. The idea of firing someone because he or she didn't show respect some considered important was an anathema

---

80. One person at Mellon told me about this time, "Decide what you want to do and then tell your presidents Mellon said you have to do it." I didn't think telling the presidents that Mellon said Tony had to continue to lead the Central Library was wise. Their reaction might have been to fire me.

to me. I would have loved to have half a dozen employees who worked as hard and accomplished as much as Tony, even if they did not stand up and salute when one of the college presidents or I entered the room. I think the presidents were shocked that Tony thought that money he and the Central Library were saving the colleges should be returned to the ACA for the expansion of those services.[81] That plan seemed reasonable to me, but I could understand how desperate most of the ACA presidents were to save money—and keep the savings.

Al Smith was a KY Hall of Fame journalist who led the Appalachian Regional Commission in D.C. and then moderated "Comment on Kentucky" for Kentucky Educational Television for thirty-three years. He spent much of his life in Appalachia and preached, at least to me, the importance of hiring employees who were indigenous Appalachians and then nurturing them by couching criticism in terms that did not disparage those who typically had low self-esteem. Understanding the culture, he believed, was more important to assuring success in Appalachia than academic credentials. Not only did I fail to keep a superb leader for the Central Library, but also, I failed to follow Al's advice and hired someone whose credentials impressed me. I didn't even follow the advice I mentioned when making my first hire at the Berea office: hire someone recommended by someone you know and trust.[82]

---

81. Expectations of the presidents were never clear, but it was clear when an employee did not meet them. The one time an employee indicated to one of the presidents on the Executive Committee that her assignment was to do whatever I told her to do, that president told me to fire her. He expected a clear list of expectations, not a general category. Complaints about Tony's attitude were frequent enough for me to conclude that the major problem many of the presidents had with his role at the ACA was that he was listening to the librarians, not the presidents. (And in some cases, the librarians were listening to Tony and not the presidents.)

82. Al referred to me as "a beggar for beggars."

After Tony left, the ACA librarians wanted to do a national search, so we hired a search firm specializing in finding librarians for new positions and ended up with two candidates being recommended: one who had been librarian at a major state university and one who was librarian at one of the private colleges in the ACA. I made the final decision and hired the woman with experience at a major university. The new hire remained until I retired and then seemed to grow frustrated with the slow speed of the ACA librarians in understanding the latest technological resources for academic libraries, or perhaps she just did not like working for the new ACA president. For whatever reason, she left and the staff person who had assisted Tony and his replacement became the director of the William G. Bowen Central Library of Appalachia.

Technology in Teaching

The Central Library emphasized the need for more and better technology at most of the ACA colleges. When I left UK, dues based on the number of full-time students at each campus were established to provide financial support for the ACA overhead. Dues for each campus were nominal, and the ACA presidents fought to keep the dues low. They were never willing to pay to support a particular program of the ACA until the Central Library was developed. But they still wanted to pay less than they were saving—regardless of how valuable the new resources might be.

As Tony explained in his review of the development of the BCLA, "The whole project raised the need for internet connections in the libraries to a much higher level of campus concern. This is particularly noteworthy on those campuses where this type of consideration was not a concern at all previously." And it was not just the librarians who had been forced to ignore the progress being made in the world of technology; they were "forced to ignore" technology because most knew that the costs associated with bringing a college campus—even a small one—to the level of bandwidth and other resources needed to access the internet adequately would be prohibitive. With the exceptions of the University of the South, Berea, and perhaps one or two others, the campuses had virtually no "smart classrooms" or if there was one, there was only one. But it was not the faculty or administrators of the ACA colleges that called attention to how critical training, equipment, and better connectivity to the internet was to the success of the ACA colleges; it was Tish Emerson.

After the move from UK, Tish contacted me to say that Mellon was going to hire a consultant to determine where our member colleges were in their use of technology in the classroom. Later, she called to say that with thirty-seven colleges and most consultants wanting $1,000 per day, getting a good report for the Mellon board was not going to be easy. Also, she had contacted one consultant whom Mellon was seriously interested in hiring only to have the consultant ask, "Where is Berea on the scale of how the colleges use technology to teach?" Tish replied, "They are near the top." The consultant then said, "Well, you're wasting your money; if Berea is near the top, the others are so far behind they will never catch up." Tish said that Mellon still was interested in helping the schools with the use of technology, but she was not sure how they were going to do that.

Shortly after that conversation with Tish, Roy Vignes called me. Roy had been a student at UK assigned to help me learn to use various computer programs. He was brilliant at anything having to do with the computer and loved working with faculty from our participating colleges. Duncan McBride, from NSF, and he developed a grant request that seemed destined to be funded until someone from the UK Math Department wrote another proposal and attached the one written by Roy as an appendix.

Roy had no patience for study in the general liberal arts, so it took him quite a while to graduate. His call to me came just after he had graduated and he was hoping that a college in the ACA would hire him. Since it was December when he called, I said that I doubted any of the colleges were hiring at that time of year, but the ACA might hire him to do a study. I asked him how much he would charge to complete a study over the next six months on the use of computers in teaching at ACA colleges; his response was about $20,000 including expenses.

I called Bob Watson, director of NSF's Division of Undergraduate Education and told him I needed $20,000 to prepare a study so the ACA could apply for funding to promote the use of technology in teaching. His response was, "So you want NSF to give you money so you can apply for more money?" When I said "Yes," he said, "Let's start this conversation over." I said, "We need to do a study," and Bob said, "Stop there; a study we can fund. We have about $19,500 left from another project; do you want that?" That question was unnecessary; of course, I wanted that.

Roy moved to an inexpensive motel in Berea and rented a car. Roy was the epitome of "thrifty." When he needed a haircut, he had his head shaved; he had two pairs of jeans and two tee-shirts that he washed until they began to fade; then he bought two more sets. His expense reports included meals, but if he had bought dessert, he insisted on paying for that himself since it wasn't really a requirement for a meal.

The Appalachian College Association (1990-2008)

When he was in the office between visits to the colleges, we had a sign on the door: "Yes, we are open 24/7." I once invited him to go to a movie with my husband and me; he refused the invitation. When I said, "You can't do nothing but work," he replied, "But that is what I like to do." When I asked when he slept, he said he "napped" and pointed out that Einstein favored napping.

After he had collected data for several months, Roy went home to Louisiana to write the report. I had not seen the final copy until he brought copies for everyone to the annual meeting of deans and presidents. I wasn't even at the session where he distributed the report and made comments about what he had learned—the major one being that the reason most of the colleges were far behind the norm in using computer technology was few of the presidents supported that use and few would fund the technology and equipment required. I remember being amazed at how well this timid computer geek held up before the vocal criticisms of the presidents after his presentation; most seriously resented being criticized for failure to fund what was becoming a critical asset in higher education, and they vocally criticized Roy as being incompetent for the task he was assigned. Nevertheless, that report circulated among various funders and helped in raising several million dollars for technology training and support.

As I noted earlier, I don't remember ever understanding much of Roy's report. So, when I wrote a request for a million dollars to help the colleges incorporate technology into their teaching, Tish called and asked me to revise it. When I rewrote it, she called and said, "All you keep saying is that you need a million dollars to help the colleges prepare their faculty to teach with technology; you don't say **how** you will help them." My response was, "But, Tish, all I can promise is that I will do something to help the faculty improve their teaching and that it will have something to do with technology."

When the ACA received the check for a million dollars, I called the graduate dean at VA Tech (who was on the Fellowship Review Committee) and asked her if she knew anyone at VA Tech who might like to lead a project preparing faculty from small colleges to use technology in their teaching. She mentioned Norm Dodle, who was just retiring from VA Tech as chair of Instructional Technology. When I sent the proposal to Norm, he called and said he would like to direct the project but I had only built $50,000 into the budget for the salary of a project director, and he had been making over $100,000, and the University would not let him work on the Tech campus (where he had the resources, including graduate students, he needed for the project) for less than $100,000.

I replied, "That's not a problem. We can make the position half-time."

"Well, I do want to spend some time fishing," he responded.

"Great," I said, "just be sure to take your cell phone when you fish—and don't take any other part-time jobs."

Norm, with lots of help from graduate students at VA Tech, scheduled multiple workshops for faculty from ACA colleges, most to be held over a weekend. At the presidents' meeting that year, one of the presidents expressed shock when he saw the $250,000 the ACA had sent to VA Tech. My response was, "And that was less than $250 per faculty member that received training, including meals and housing."

At the end of the two-year project funding training in technology,

Norm said he wanted to hold a Technology Summit to display what the faculty had learned. I was concerned because I had no idea what they had learned; for all I knew they were copying web sources illegally. Norm said, "Trust me," and I did. The University of TN gave us their conference center for the two-day event. Randy Bass from Georgetown University was the keynote speaker; at that time he had asked his university to delay his request for tenure because he was doing so much that was experimental in the classroom he knew the review committee would not see him as a promising scholar. But since that ACA conference in the late 1990s, he has become recognized as a world-famous scholar in the field, leading such experiments as the Visible Knowledge Project, where he worked for five years with seventy faculty from twenty-one universities on the scholarship of learning. The ACA Summit attracted so many faculty that we had to send Bass's presentation electronically to a room outside the auditorium where he was speaking. Later, he ran a workshop at Georgetown for ACA faculty. Here was the kind of experience that I wanted to provide for ACA faculty—including participants who were comfortable with each other and presenters who were leaders in their academic fields.

The next day, after visiting various presentations by ACA faculty, Tish Emerson came to me and said, "If you can do this with one million, let's see what you can do with four million." And the Summit has been offered every year since, at least up until this memoir was written. Attendance varied little, generally attracting about four hundred participants each year. My only disappointment in the Summit was that it became less and less focused on technology and more and more focused on pedagogy. And, I had learned that Mellon, the major funder of the Summit, wanted little or none of their money spent on pedagogy,[83] unless that training focused on learning new ways to use technology in teaching.

A Teaching and Learning Institute (TLI) began in 2003 in which forty-seven faculty from twenty-one ACA colleges gathered for a week at Brevard College to review teaching strategies and collaborate regarding learning, assessment, service learning, using technology to teach, and construction of syllabi. At the second Institute, sixty-five faculty from twenty-eight colleges participated. Like the Summit, this event has been repeated every summer since I retired. One piece of data I remember from evaluations of the TLI is that just under fifty percent of the participants said their deans ever emphasized issues discussed at the institutes while eighty percent of the deans said they did.

Norm assumed that since he was working with faculty and students of the member colleges, the ACA college presidents would support his suggestions for incorporating technology into teaching on their campuses. Clearly, training faculty to use technology made little sense if the facilities and equipment, as well as some local assistance with the technology, were not available. When Norm learned of the problems faculty who completed one of the VA Tech workshops were having when they returned to their home institutions and found that not only were there too few computers on their campuses, but also the electrical systems wouldn't support many more, he suggested that he should meet with the trustees of the colleges (as a group) to stress the importance of upgrading the institutional technology. He believed that if trustees understood the importance of instructional technology, campus budgets would include funding increases for it.

---

83. See paragraph two in the introduction to the section on History of the Appalachian College Program.

But the presidents were adamant that their trustees would not meet with trustees across the ACA to discuss technology or any other topic. When I asked "Why?" the response was, "If my trustees meet the trustees at Berea, they may come back to me wanting to know why our college is not doing what Berea is doing." Most of the thirty-seven (at that time) colleges were struggling to keep their lights on. The presidents did not want their colleges to be compared with a college with an endowment approaching a billion dollars. Similarly, there was no interest in offering alumni from multiple colleges the chance to travel together. Encouraging alumni from one college to talk to those from another might result in the alumni from one college making donations to a college other than their alma mater.

Unfortunately, our success with four million dollars was less than that we anticipated based on the success we had experienced with one million dollars. First, in the early years of our attempt to increase the use of technology at ACA colleges, we were working with faculty who had little or no experience in working with technology. It was easy to see the improvements a short workshop could produce. In later years, we were working with faculty who knew the basics, but had little support on their own campuses to learn more; in fact, in many cases faculty could not incorporate what they had learned into their classrooms because their campuses lacked the technology infrastructure needed to do so. Second, Norm retired. Third, our goals became much more ambitious with the second grant; for example, one goal was to provide a centralized course management system for all ACA colleges.

The ACA deans insisted that we do a national search for Norm's replacement, and we did such a search, even flying someone from

Alaska to Berea for an interview. A person I had met at a Salzburg seminar related to technology, a recent graduate from the University of Chicago, came for an interview. When I offered him the job, promising to match his salary at his job in Chicago, he turned it down. When I asked him why, he said, "There are no bars in Berea." Apparently, bars are a critical asset to single young men.

We hired one of Norm's graduate students at VA Tech, but she lacked the expertise and authority Norm had held as a long-time department chair. She could not call a colleague at VA Tech and schedule meeting rooms and tech support for an ACA conference at no cost; she had to go through the various channels developed for those new in their positions. Then, after several months on the job, when she had discovered how much traveling she needed to do to be successful in working with ACA faculty, and how, as a single mother, she often needed to leave her teenage children alone, she emailed me her resignation.

Another hire was a woman from Eastern KY University who had provided tech support for one of the departments and felt slighted by the fact that those working in academic departments helping faculty with technology did not make as much or enjoy the prestige of those working in the central technology office. This new hire stayed about six months. She was completely unprepared for the workload. My daughter's college dorm had a sign near her room that read, "If you're not happy here, you probably won't be happy anywhere." I tried to remember that when hiring future staff: if they weren't happy in their previous job, it is likely they wouldn't be happy at the ACA.

At some point, I learned that Martin Ramsay, who was heading the technology center at Berea College, was leaving his position. (Berea had a new president and I could relate to the problem with new bosses.) I asked him if he wanted to come to work for the ACA. He had been a successful consultant before going to work for Berea and wanted to continue to consult; we agreed that he could consult two days each month—the agreement I understood he had with Berea College. Martin was not only knowledgeable about technology, he was also skilled at writing proposals and reports.

For a year or so, Martin proved to be a major asset for the ACA—although he believed in building consensus, which I found often a slow way to make progress. I once watched him spend four hours (after dinner) reaching agreement on which equipment would be most valuable for ACA colleges involved in one of his assigned projects. He wanted everyone in that room to know why a particular choice was made. I would have taken a vote and not worried too much about those who did not fit into the outcome of the majority. But I was impressed with Martin's relationship with the faculty, deans, and computer staff across the ACA campuses. When I had agreed he could consult outside the office for two days a month, what I did not specify was that he could not carry forward more than two months of consulting days. By carrying forward even three months, he could be consulting out of the office for over a week.

When Martin began to utilize the days for consulting that he had accumulated and was out of the ACA office for multiple days at a time, I realized how critical he was to the office. As I found myself taking an increasing number of phone calls from people asking for a reference for Martin, whom they were considering hiring as a consultant, I realized I had made a major mistake in including permission for him to consult in his employment agreement.

I met with Martin to discuss his options: (1) he could continue to work for the ACA but only on a full-time basis, or (2) he could resign from the ACA and consult full-time with the understanding that when the ACA needed his talents, he could be hired as a consultant.[84] He chose to leave, but he oversaw the annual Summit until a year after my retirement, and he continues to lead the Learning Asset Management Project (LAMP) which started at the ACA but continued as an independent, self-supporting consortium after the grant funding ended. Martin reminded me that after I retired the ACA had received a $50,000 award for his work with technology, but he thought the ACA returned the money to Mellon.

Following is the list Martin sent to reflect the projects he assisted or oversaw for the ACA during his years in the office:

- *TIIAP (Technology Information Infrastructure Assistance Program funded by the US Department of Commerce). Eight ACA colleges did eight different projects to bring technology to their communities. For example, WV Wesleyan sat up a computer lab in the lobby of a local motel to give computer access to people in the community in one of the few places in the area that was open 24/7.*

- *Technology Fellowships. Mellon funds provided faculty with opportunities to explore ways to use technology in their teaching and research.*

- *Tech Summit. Large annual gatherings of ACA faculty were held*

---

84. Martin remembered the reason he decided to leave the ACA was because the grant funding his position was ending. It was, but Martin was so versatile that he could probably have filled an important position on another grant. When Martin wrote to say his version of why he left the ACA was different from mine, he added, "This manuscript is your memoir—not mine; you need to write what you remember."

to display and discuss their use of technology for teaching and learning. These three-day events eventually became opportunities for faculty and students to demonstrate new approaches to teaching and research; and they have continued to the current day.

- IT Directors Meetings. These Mellon-funded workshops were designed to bring more professionalism to IT departments at ACA member institutions.

- Student Technology Assistants (STAs). This project developed an excellent curriculum to train students to provide technical support for their campuses. It was funded by a grant from Jessie Ball duPont Fund that was awarded to VA Tech. Small grants were available to students trained at Tech to develop new teaching materials for faculty at their home colleges.[85]

- Once the grant ended, the ACA staff continued to offer the weekend workshops for students to become tech support, but with the ACA directing the training programs at ACA colleges, there were not the unanticipated benefits noted when Tech was involved. These unanticipated benefits had included: (1) the students returned to their home colleges convinced that since they had been able to help Tech faculty, they could certainly help faculty on their own campuses, and (2) faculty at the ACA colleges were convinced that students with certification from Tech in technology assistance were professionally qualified to help them.

---

85. The ACA was not eligible to apply to duPont, but VA Tech could apply to administer a grant to serve ACA colleges. Later, UNC-Chapel Hill submitted a grant to duPont to fund a project designed to work with selected ACA colleges on economic development in their local communities.

- *Instructional Technology Assistants (ITAs). Piggybacking off the success of the STA program, ITAs attended training together with a faculty member. These faculty-ITA pairs learned many different kinds of technology that were useful for instructional design.*

- *Packet Shapers. Many schools were beginning to experience problems with their limited bandwidth being outstripped by the demand. We provided packet shaper devices that allowed schools to throttle some kinds of (often non-academic) internet traffic while giving precedence to academic traffic. I assisted Rob Hoyt in this effort.*

- *Comparative Analysis. I developed a rather sophisticated method of collecting data about ACA member schools and then presenting the data in a way that maintained individual school anonymity but that allowed comparison between schools in many dimensions: financial, student demographics, admissions, technology, and more. The presidents and deans were pleased enough to continue paying for the collecting and reporting this data in the format I developed for five years after I left the ACA.*

- *Element K. We provided web-based training on a wide host of topics from programming to Microsoft office tools and beyond.*

- *Learning Management System. Initially a Mellon grant allowed us to provide WebCT, the (then) premier Learning Management System (LMS). It was very expensive, and we attempted (rather unsuccessfully) to host it ourselves. At the end of the grant period, the schools did not have any money to keep it going. After extensive meetings and "test drives," we built the LAMP Consortium that was a financially self-supporting community*

> based on the open source LMS platform, Sakai. The LAMP Consortium is no longer a part of the ACA, but it continues to thrive to this day with twenty-one colleges participating, some members of the ACA and others outside the region.

Martin was not the only employee hired to help the member colleges address technology needs; another was Rob Hoyt, who had worked with the ACA as technology support staff when he was a student at Berea College. For a while after he graduated, he was a full-time ACA employee. Rob sent me a compilation of his work at the ACA as well as copies of some of the ACA annual reports produced when I was president there. Rob's wife, Emily, worked, after she graduated from Berea College, as an assistant in my office. They were two of the best employees I ever had, but not long after they came to work for me, Emily's father became critically ill, and they returned to Iowa to help take care of the family. Rob has, I understand, continued to work in technology, writing software programs for agricultural purposes and developing software to help businesses keep expenses under control.

Following is Rob's summary of his work with the ACA:

> It almost seems like a past life at this point, but as I recall, when I came to the ACA for the first time it was as a student worker for Berea College to support the single, small computer that was onsite providing email for the staff at the ACA office and to get a better understanding of what the ACA would need from the college in the future.

> By the time I left the ACA, we were hosting somewhere around twenty advanced servers and the network infrastructure to support these systems. This technology provided everything from email to shared course management, as well as many services for the Central

Library program. We had two full-time positions, mine and that of a Systems Administrator, as well as a student position. We spent most of our time doing two things:

First, building and maintaining the infrastructure and support system to allow the ACA to host collaborative services for the member institutions as well as supporting the growing staff and programs being offered to the institutions.

Second, creating a more involved network of IT administrators and decision makers on each campus in order to better understand what the above "collaborative services" might need to be, and quite frankly how we could help them without creating more work than the generally overloaded staff members already had.

Probably not an inclusive list but many of the important services we hosted were:

- *ACA Email Services*
- *ACA Website*
- *ACA List Server*
- *Digital Library of Appalachia*
- *ERES Library Web Server*
- *Library Proxy Servers*
- *WebCT Shared Course Management.*

As Martin mentioned, when I first started with the ACA there was very little involvement with the member institution IT departments to include them in collaborative functions. While I was at the ACA, several key IT leaders from the member institutions started the ITCG (Information Technology Collaborative Group); and it was through this group that many of the collaborations came to fruition. I believe it is through this group that we facilitated the group purchasing opportunities, such as the Packet Shaper devices that Martin mentioned and Web Caching servers, as well as the annual IT meetings where the content and vendor presence was directed more specifically to information technology administrators, technicians, and student assistants.

It was also around this time that we began to organize specific tracks and sessions for the annual Tech Summit which were technical in nature in order to entice IT personnel to attend. The hope was that they would become involved in the other sessions to offer advice and planning for collaborative projects that would undoubtedly require their involvement on their local campus.

Based in part on the model of the Central Library where joint purchasing enabled ACA colleges to have access to resources few of the individual colleges could have afforded to purchase individually and working with Element K (which provided online training in topics such as Microsoft Word, Excel, PowerPoint, Adobe Photoshop, Illustrator, Dreamweaver, and roughly 1,500 other courses), over 3,700 licenses were purchased for training staff and faculty and supporting technology help desks.[86]

In the early years of the work the ACA did to help facilitate the use of technology in teaching, Berea College provided support for those efforts. The college hosted a server for the use of the ACA office until

---

86. Rob was a bit nervous when he learned that Ira Fuchs, the computer expert from the Mellon office, was going to attend one of the ACA's Summits. But Ira was highly complimentary of Rob and his work; his assessment was that the ACA colleges were having the same problems incorporating technology into teaching as almost every other college. In fact, Ira mentioned that there might be a position in New York for someone with Rob's credentials.

traffic for the ACA office increased, and the ACA purchased its own server. As activities and staffing related to the technology projects increased, Berea College provided office space for the ACA staff working on those efforts. Unfortunately, without a major institution providing expertise and equipment to support the efforts of our small ACA office to help the member colleges obtain and monitor technology so it could be incorporated into teaching, the impact of the ACA efforts related to technology could not achieve what the small colleges in rural Appalachia needed. It was unrealistic for the ACA to even try to bring over thirty colleges into the new world of teaching with technology. Most of the colleges needed an infrastructure which we could not give them, and they could not afford on their own. But we certainly supported a lot of individuals struggling to use at least some technology that could enhance their teaching, and we certainly made a lot of presidents aware of what they were providing or denying their students in terms of the use of technologies that would help them in any field after they graduated.

Collaboration Across Colleges

Most ACA projects supported faculty and/or students for individual research or study. With some evidence that collaboration was successful with groups of faculty, the following projects were part of an effort to develop institutional commitments to collaboration.

One project supported by Mellon was designed to move collaboration by individuals to institutional collaboration. While the funding was intended to motivate presidents to get more involved in planning collaborative projects across ACA colleges, it was typically administrative staff or faculty who developed the ideas. I once took three ACA presidents to dinner and said to them, "There is $40,000 in the middle of this table that you can take home with you if you can come up with one idea that will lead to collaborations across your campuses." They couldn't. Each president was convinced that his college was unique, even when I pointed out that if I put the mission statements of all thirty-seven of the ACA colleges on a table, few of the presidents could identify his or hers. There was only one statement that didn't mention "Christian values."

Every faculty member seemed to believe his style of teaching was uniquely fitted to the students of that institution in a way that couldn't be captured by another faculty member at another college. Tish once suggested the ACA colleges should offer online courses such as physics and calculus taught by faculty at Princeton or University of Pennsylvania. Even I thought that would never work. Most ACA students lack self-confidence; they would never believe they could do well in a course taught by someone unfamiliar with the weaknesses that come from being educated in a community of poverty. Also, collaboration was difficult to promote in a region where college presidents prided themselves on independence.

During this time, someone at VA Tech offered to let students at ACA colleges take their online courses related to technology. I was surprised to learn there was only one course that covered basic technology skills; it offered one hour of credit.[87] My understanding was that no tuition would change hands; VA Tech would charge the ACA a small fee for

---

87. Perhaps most students entered VA Tech with basic computer skills.

each student from an ACA college who enrolled, and the ACA would add that amount to the college's annual fee. Each student taking a Tech course was to have a tutor at his or her own campus to help with questions that might arise, and the student's grade could be determined by that tutor, based on the standards of that college, not on those of VA Tech. Only one ACA college took advantage of the course—once. When I asked an ACA president why he did not want his school to participate, he said, "I don't want my students taking a course from VA Tech; they may decide they like Tech so much they will transfer to it." My response was, "Or some of the VA Tech students in the course might hear your students talking about your college and decide to transfer to it." At least he did not say what I had heard dozens of times: "Students don't come to my college to sit in front of a computer."[88]

This claim to being unique among ACA colleges became an issue when I tried to get the colleges to advertise job openings collectively. One major job listing in the *Chronicle of Higher Education* could recruit multiple teachers for courses in the same disciplines across ACA colleges. Similarly, the response to jointly recruiting students was that every college was different from the others. The attitude did not change even after I explained that if we had a central office that was seeing the applications, when a college rejected an applicant, we might be able to find another in the ACA network that would accept the student.[89]

While the ACA office was still at UK, several colleges had explored the possibility of teaching foreign languages using interactive classrooms

---

88. With COVID-19, a lot of colleges may wish today (2020) that they had spent more time preparing their faculty and students for online education.

89. What I was suggesting was similar to the Common Application process available today.

and a teacher who could hold various sessions across the participating colleges. When Tish Emerson came to observe one of the programs, I apologized because "the project failed." Tish's response was, "No, the technology failed." There had been some national crises on the day the demonstration took place, and the internet was full of traffic related to that emergency, pushing out efforts related to the language instruction.

At one point the public relations staff across the colleges organized a professional development workshop that attracted twenty-five people from twelve ACA colleges. One event for this group included five guest speakers from places like *USA Today* and the editor of *University Business* magazine. What I remember from the presentations by major media representatives was their comments about how the national news agencies are not interested in what is happening at one small school in VA; they want to know what is happening across lots of colleges. The media staff from across multiple ACA colleges never followed up on identifying general issues that might warrant broad publicity—once again illustrating that without a strong leader to dedicate time to promoting a project, many good ideas die. And a major problem at ACA colleges, where the teaching load is high and other responsibilities are numerous, is the limitations on time to be creative.

Perhaps I should have formed a consortium of funders; they were in touch with me more often than the presidents or deans of the ACA colleges. The Advisory Council was close to being a consortium; many members had experience working with foundations and federal agencies. They provided guidance I could never get from the ACA presidents, and they were able to consider ideas that could benefit every college in the ACA, some more than others, but always in a way that touched every institution interested in participating.

Summaries of Other Projects Funded Between 1993-2008

Projects Promoting Institutional Collaboration (Mellon): (1) a central Human Resources office for WV colleges (which closed once grant funds were no longer providing much of the salary for staff at the office); (2) a workshop held at the University of Pennsylvania's Wharton School of Business where ACA college representatives identified new areas for collaboration, including a web-based strategy for communicating with young alumni of the participating colleges and collaboration across the campuses to provide career development and placement offices; (3) a collaborative program for orientation of new faculty from multiple ACA colleges based on the program Berea College provides for new faculty, including a trip of several days through eastern Kentucky, stopping at schools, clinics, churches, and homes so new faculty can see the environment in which most Berea College students have been reared; (4) a well-attended seminar related to international studies to help ACA colleges understand the risks as well as the benefits of such programs; and (5) programs developed to host visiting artists across multiple ACA colleges and to promote the *Nantahala Review*, an online periodical which won a prize from the Appalachian Studies Association for its presentation of works of art in Appalachia.

Other Projects that encouraged collaborative research and study, if not institutional collaboration, included the following:

The Independent College Enterprise (ICE) (Mellon): ICE is a program developed under a Mellon grant encouraging collaboration. ICE is housed at the University of Charleston in West Virginia. The purpose of the program was to share back-office technology resources and consolidate operating functions where practical. Funding from Mellon enabled the presidents to develop the strategy for consolidating back-office functions, but the West Virginia college presidents (and a couple outside WV) provided the funding for the equipment, training, and software, and ICE has continued to operate as an independent non-profit organization. Both LAMP, the consortium of over twenty colleges that share an operating system, and the Independent College Enterprise (ICE) office providing shared back-offices systems now operate independent of the ACA with fees or dues being paid by participating institutions in each program.

Appalachian Watershed Studies (Mellon; NSF): Mellon funds supported a collaboration between the Appalachian Laboratory[90] and Ferrum, Sewanee, Lindsey Wilson, King, Montreat, and WV Wesleyan (all ACA colleges). ACA faculty participated in research in aquatic ecology, landscape and watershed ecology, conservation biology and restoration ecology, behavioral and evolutionary ecology, and ecosystems across Appalachia. A major NSF grant helped establish CAWS (Collaboration through Appalachian Watershed Studies) whereby research and workshops were held for faculty and students at ACA colleges. Shortly after I retired, EREN (Ecological Research as Education) was formed with ACA faculty from Sewanee and Ferrum serving as board representatives. EREN currently has over 300 member institutions across the US and in several foreign countries. In 2010, EREN received an NSF grant of almost $500,000.

Salzburg Seminars (Mellon): Shortly after World War II, as *Wikipedia*

---

90. Located in Frostburg, MD, as an institute within the University System of Maryland known as Appalachian Watershed Studies.

explains, some students from Harvard challenged "present and future leaders to solve issues of global concern" through programs held in Salzburg and in other locations throughout the world. Since 1947, more than five hundred sessions consisting of more than 30,000 participants from one hundred sixty nine countries have been held. In the late 1990s, Mellon program officers saw the Salzburg programs could serve faculty at the small, isolated colleges in central Appalachia, and invited a proposal to fund faculty for sessions at Schloss Leopoldskron, a palace in Salzburg. Topics for discussions by participants from multiple countries have included education, health care, economics, geopolitics, justice, and sustainability. In some cases, the entire program was designated for ACA participants, but usually the ACA participants joined other scholars from around the world. It is no surprise that the opportunity to attend these seminars was repeatedly mentioned by faculty in describing major benefits of ACA membership.

Women in Leadership Positions (Mellon): Several women at Mellon expressed concern when they learned that there were no women presidents at ACA colleges and only six or so chief academic officers who were women. To address that concern, funding was provided for projects designed to identify women at ACA colleges interested in college administration and encourage them through workshops which were related to career advancement (a total of one hundred seventy attended). Some women attended the Higher Education Resource Services (HERS) Summer Institute held at Bryn Mawr. It was fascinating that the response to the first survey sent to determine the professional interests of women employed at ACA colleges had a return rate that was higher than the number of surveys sent; apparently women receiving the surveys made copies to distribute to women who had not received one from the ACA office.⁹¹ It was also interesting that in every survey submitted asking the presidents to rank ACA programs in terms of their importance, Women in Administration came last. However, thanks to the commitment to support women that was exhibited by Mellon staff, we were able to give each woman who was an academic dean a small grant to hold workshops on developing leadership skills for women, including students, on their campuses.⁹²

Alumni Outcomes Survey: Comparison of Graduates from ACA Colleges and from Regional Universities (Spencer and Mellon): This study was led by Ernest Pascarella and Pat Terenzini, well-known scholars focusing on the impact of higher education on students. Results were published in a report called "In the Shadow of the Mountains." The researchers surveyed graduates from ACA colleges and from five state universities in the region, looking at outcomes of their college experiences five, ten, and twenty years after graduation. Included were core educational outcomes: moral, personal, and character development; career and occupational preparation; quality of life; and outcomes in six other areas. ACA alumni reported a greater impact of their undergraduate experience on personal and spiritual development and responsible citizenship, increased overall satisfaction with college, deeper religious involvement and a higher

---

91. The constantly changing directories of faculty at the ACA colleges created problems for the ACA staff trying to maintain a general directory of all faculty across the network. We continued to depend on the academic deans to distribute information about ACA benefits; some were more diligent in fulfilling this assignment than others.

92. The numbers of women academic deans and presidents at ACA colleges have certainly increased since these efforts to prepare women for leadership positions, but I did hear stories about ongoing efforts to keep women "in their place." One woman told me that when she went to her president to tell him what she had learned at HERS, he told her that she "was not going to blackmail him into giving her a promotion."

percentage of income donated to charity, and a greater likelihood of working in the Appalachian region. The public university graduates reported higher salaries and greater use of technology, and there were minor differences in educational attainment, satisfaction with their lives, and engaging in life-long learning. The final report might be of interest for a similar study on more recent graduates; the report on this 2003 study should be in the archives of the ACA—or at the University of Iowa in the office of Dr. Pascarella. If neither of those offices can provide a copy of the report, the Spencer Foundation or The Andrew W. Mellon Foundation might be able to provide copies.

ACA Research Fellows (Spencer): Thirteen research fellows from nine ACA colleges worked with Pascarella and Terenzini to identify research questions that could be answered with data from the alumni study. Three meetings were held to discuss the design and scope of the alumni study and to develop follow-up research questions. Topics included social capital, mobility, and class; women's issues; effects on behavior; influences of student debt; and completion of graduate degrees. With Pascarella's base at the University of Iowa, where he had access to ACT records, researchers were able to find pre-college information (ACT scores, majors planned, etc.) to compare with outcomes data.

Studying the Arts (McCune): Fred Mullinax had worked with the McCune Foundation in Pittsburgh when he was president at Alice Lloyd College. That foundation had once funded Alice Lloyd, Cumberland College, and several other ACA colleges, but the McCune trustees had determined they wanted to limit their giving to fewer nonprofits. Fred visited Martha Perry, a program officer he knew at McCune, and asked if the McCune board would consider funding the ACA at least as a transition grant, giving access to grant funds to thirty-seven colleges when McCune would only have one grant to administer. Some of the major (i.e., over a million dollars) McCune grants supported the fellowship endowment for faculty in education and other professional fields (Wilma Dykeman Fellowships) and the arts (Jean Ritchie Fellowships).

Other memorable grants from McCune came when the board members declared they wanted to restrict funding to Pittsburgh agencies. Martha offered an idea: McCune could fund the ACA so faculty from member colleges could travel to Pittsburgh (flying on Pittsburgh-based US Air), spend several nights in a local Pittsburgh hotel, have meals at Pittsburgh restaurants, and attend workshops related to Pittsburgh arts organizations, such as the Pittsburgh Opera. Those grants lasted for several years and study at the Opera included such topics as how to relate the liberal arts to teaching opera; for example, a physics faculty member from Davidson College taught a course on how physics is related to understanding opera—and vice versa. After several years of sending faculty to Pittsburgh, the Opera Company sent their interns to tour across central Appalachia, performing mini operas at various ACA colleges.

Several years ago, when the McCune Foundation held over $300 million, the board started to award Sunset Grants to spend-down the funding and close the foundation by 2029. It is sad to think about ending a foundation that has served so many non-profit organizations so well.

Faculty/Student Traveling Art Exhibitions and Workshops (Alf Canon Fund): Funding that remained at Warren Wilson after the ACA office moved from there was placed in a fund named the Alf Canon Fund to honor Dr. Canon for his work with the ACA. The first project funded by the Alf Canon Fund was an exhibit of paintings produced by faculty and students from across the ACA. In the fall of 2001, four ACA colleges hosted exhibits and in the spring and fall of 2002 five different colleges hosted exhibits. Two colleges hosted workshops on developing various art styles. The costs for the exhibits and the workshops were nominal, and I expected they would continue with a different type of art being featured each year, but no one took the lead on that idea, so it never happened during my tenure.

Community Service Grants: Developing Citizen Scholars (Surdna Foundation): Faculty at ACA colleges during the time the office was at UK frequently wanted to use Mellon grants for community service. I explained that Mellon was interested in academic research and graduate study, not community service. Then Steve Fisher, an Emory & Henry faculty member, came to me with a proposal for "participatory research" in which students and faculty would go to a rural community and work with those there to study such topics as the history of the town, the development of local industries, and water quality issues. I agreed to fund the project but stressed that the final report needed to focus on how much the students and faculty learned, not how much good they had done. Still, the final report was primarily evidence of how grateful the local residents were for the help they had received. I said then that no more Mellon funds could go for projects that did not focus exclusively on academic research and study. Fortunately, after the move to Berea, a friend of Tish, Elizabeth Grubbs, convinced the Surdna Foundation to fund Citizen Scholars, allowing students at ACA colleges to work with faculty and community service agencies to provide help for their communities and disadvantaged people within them. The grant was funded in 2005 and fifty-four students from fourteen ACA colleges received

Citizen Scholars grants during the 2006-2007 year.[93]

Entrepreneurship in Appalachia (Appalachian Regional Commission): This grant provided funding for ACA faculty to collaborate across campuses to develop an online course on entrepreneurship skills that could be used at all the ACA colleges.

Distinguished Scholars (NSF): NSF awarded $270,000 for scholarships to as many as forty graduates of Appalachian high schools who were at ACA colleges majoring in C-STEM subjects (computer science, technology, engineering, and math). The scholarship funds could be used to pay tuition and purchase books, supplies, and equipment. When the graduate deans from the six major research universities in the region met to review fellowship applications, these undergraduate scholars often met with those deans to talk about graduate school opportunities. The dean from the University of Tennessee said she was hesitant to tell the students that the largest graduate school fellowship she could offer was about $12,000—until one of the students said, "You mean I can get **paid** to go to graduate school?" At other ACA meetings, such as the Summit, the students also heard from representatives of industries and professional associations regarding job opportunities in Appalachia.

STEM Scholarships (NSF): Forty-seven students from eighteen ACA colleges received $6,000 scholarships in 2006-2007 to major in STEM fields. The hope was that these students would explore career opportunities in Appalachia and build the entrepreneurial capacity

---

93. Funding from both McCune and Surdna came as the result of people outside the ACA making connections with funders the ACA had never contacted. In fact, those of us in the office had never heard of them until they were prepared to discuss a grant for the ACA.

of the region.

Robert C. Noyce Scholarships (NSF): These scholarships were awarded to encourage students who have strong backgrounds in science and math to work toward a teaching certificate and teach after graduation in a school that needs more science and math teachers. The NSF grant provided funds to support fifty-four scholarships of $7,500.[94]

International Study (Berger Foundation and Christian A. Johnson): Fred Mullinax, former president of Alice Lloyd College, developed a program which allowed faculty to submit proposals for international study with students. He raised the funding for it, oversaw the application process, and monitored final reports. Students received scholarships of $8,000 to spend a semester abroad with various organizations. The first year these were offered (2001-2002) fourteen students participated. Three short-term seminars took place in Europe and Asia. Topics for programs hosted by the ACA included "Global Citizenship"; "Literary and Historical Studies in London and Paris"; and "The Downfall of the Third Reich." A trip for business majors to Korea and China, led by faculty from King College, was offered in 2002. In each case, faculty from an ACA college led the experiences and students from across the ACA participated.

In addition to the multiple opportunities for international study, scholarships were available for as many as twenty students to participate in internships with the Washington Center in Washington, D.C. Hoping to build on the programs established once the funding had ended, I hired Carol de Rosset, who had led international programs

---

94. These NSF grants were first funded close to the time of my retirement, so I do not know if these early grants were funded again or even if the ACA continued to apply for the funding.

at Berea, and Nancy Lackey, who had been dean of Student Life at Centre College, to develop new ACA international programs. Within a short time, Carol grew uncomfortable with resistance of the participating colleges to honor policies developed by the ACA to help assure the safety and security of student participants. She returned to being a faculty member at Berea. Nancy was disappointed in the faculty from various colleges who were supposed to help with monitoring the students on the trips but spent most of their time being tourists rather than monitors; she left the ACA and accepted a full-time position as an assistant to the president at Centre College.

Undergraduate Research in the Humanities (Mellon): When Phil Lewis from the Mellon Foundation came to speak at one of the annual meetings of the presidents, Anne Ponder, who was on the ACA Advisory Council[95] and had just been named president of the University of North Carolina at Asheville, spoke with him about making resources at UNC-Asheville available to students at ACA colleges. Since students had multiple opportunities to do research in STEM fields, the new grant supporting ACA students and faculty to do research with UNC-Asheville faculty focused on the humanities. That grant was renewed by the researchers at UNC-Asheville at least once after I retired. Here was another example of the benefits to be derived by collaboration between private colleges and public universities.

Economic Development in Appalachia (duPont): Even the chancellor

---

95. I had served on the Board of Trustees at Colby Sawyer when Anne was president there. She told me that when I retired, she would be interested in applying for my job. I thought that was a great idea, but I also feared some of the presidents were going to hesitate to hire another strong woman. I added her to the Advisory Council so the presidents would get to know and like her by the time I retired. Then she would be in a good position to apply for my job. Unfortunately for the ACA, Anne became chancellor at UNC-Asheville the year before I retired.

at UNC-Chapel Hill endorsed the ACA when Jesse White from the Rural Development Center there submitted a proposal to Jessie Ball duPont for funding faculty at UNC-Chapel Hill to work with five of the ACA member colleges—one in each state served. The goal was to establish programs supporting the economic development of each region. The chancellor at UNC-Chapel Hill had to choose one proposal out of many submitted by various divisions of UNC to send to duPont. His endorsement of the ACA proposal was based not only on the fact that the mission of the project was clearly a worthy one, but also on the observation that working with the ACA gave UNC-Chapel Hill a new presence in five states. The Business School faculty at UNC were a bit taken aback when they learned neither Jesse nor I had built in stipends for their assistance. Jesse explained he saw working with these private colleges as part of their responsibility as faculty associated with the Rural Development Center. They did a great job but had no interest in seeking a renewal of grant funding when the project ended. Although KY Christian was unsuccessful in generating cooperation from agencies across that geographic region, the other participating colleges seem to have accomplished their goals.

Travel grants (Mellon and Pew): From the first grants funded by Mellon and Pew, one benefit was funding for expenses related to participation in appropriate discipline-related conferences or seminars. Usually, such grants were available for faculty to make a presentation at a regional or national or international conference. And many of these grants were awarded every year; each grant could take a faculty member a long way toward fulfilling his or her obligations to promote their research or to learn more in their academic fields. The ACA presidents and deans declared these grants were valuable tools for recruiting and retention of their faculty. Since the amount necessary for each award was typically low, a large number of awards could be made. For example, in the 2006-2007 academic year, $25,500 made it possible for sixty-seven faculty at twenty-six ACA colleges to be awarded grants for expenses related to their participation in professional academic events.

Small projects ($5,000 or less): Hanes, Scripps Howard, Travelers Insurance (for general support); BB&T (for a workshop on financial literacy); Nancy Sederberg's Forward Fund[96] (provided funding for women in administration to attend workshops related to professional development); and David Baldacci's Wish-You-Well Foundation (to support several Appalachian artists to tour the region and make presentations at multiple ACA colleges). Baldacci presented his gift at a meeting of ACA presidents. The meeting in which Baldacci spoke at the final luncheon of the presidents' gathering was the only one I remember where none of the ACA presidents slipped out before the final event of an annual meeting.

---

96. Nancy was chair of the Deans Council when she called to tell me she had been fired and she didn't know why. She was going to sue her college for (1) age discrimination, 2) sexual discrimination, and 3) violating the Americans with Disabilities Act. She was over fifty-five, the only woman on the President's Council, and she was just completing treatment for cancer. She said by suing the college she would never get another job in higher education; I told her she was one of the best academic deans I had known and that I would love to have her work for the ACA. I called her president to ask if he would have a problem if the ACA hired Nancy as a consultant for six months; his response was that he wouldn't have a problem if she wasn't suing. When the college's lawyer came to take my deposition, after several hours, he said the president had said he never told me that he didn't want Nancy to work for the ACA. Then he asked me if I was calling the president a liar. My response was, "I'm not telling you what he said; I'm telling you what I heard." Nancy won her case and part of the agreement was that she could write a letter of recommendation for herself that the president of the college would have to sign. She gave the ACA a small grant for projects submitted by women faculty. However, she never had a paying job in higher education again—at least not one she mentioned to me.

Another Strategic Plan

In 2003, when I announced that I would retire in five years, I quickly realized that I should have kept that plan a secret. One problem with announcing a departure date long before its implementation is that some staff who had been working diligently began to ignore my directions and worked halfheartedly when they had been exceeding my expectations in almost all of their work. When Danielle at Mellon asked me why the ACA colleges were not participating more with the National Institute for Technology in Liberal Education (NITLE), I said that I couldn't get the staff in charge of technology to make that happen. Then Danielle asked, "Why won't they respond to your direction?" The chair of the ACA Executive Committee, who was with me at the time, said, "Because they know she is leaving."

When the Executive Committee began to discuss my raise for the coming year, I explained that my salary was more than adequate (and excessive compared with what I was allowed to pay highly productive staff), but since I had led the ACA without a contract since I had been hired ten years earlier, I wanted a contract promising another five years in my position. The board approved the contract, and then arranged for deferred compensation for me since the presidents, at least some of them, insisted my salary had remained too low.[97]

Shortly after that annual meeting, some of the presidents announced they wanted to develop a strategic plan for the coming years. They were clear about wanting a subset of the presidents to develop the plan; they did not want to hire an outside consultant. Some had been

---

97. I agreed with them when I learned what my replacement would be paid.

frustrated by the work Beth Baxter had done when she developed the plan that was included with the NEH Challenge Grant application. They felt she had not listened to them but had written what she thought the ACA should accomplish. I believe she had listened carefully to each president's thoughts about the direction of the ACA and then developed a plan that incorporated as many of the major suggestions as was reasonable. Also, she had added her suggestions for improving the ACA (such as the addition of an Advisory Council; the inclusion in the annual reports of a chart reflecting benefits gained for dues paid; and fundraising for fellowships for faculty in fields other than arts and sciences, such as those in professional fields like business and in performing arts). When the Appalachian Regional Commission in Washington, D.C., recommended the ACA to the New York Community Trust as an agency that could be trusted to administer the wishes of their donors, the ACA had reached another goal Beth had listed: a national reputation. We had accomplished the recommendations Beth had made and those accomplishments had made the ACA strong and recognized as an association to be admired, if not replicated.[98]

The Strategic Planning Committee presented their plan at the next meeting of the Executive Committee prior to taking it to the full ACA Governing Board. The first recommendation was that the ACA should slow its work related to fundraising. The explanation was that "the ACA has grown too fast; we need to focus on maintaining the Association—on stabilizing it." My response was, "Those of you

---

98. Funding agencies had worked with the ACA before the presidents of the member colleges had established the independent association. Thus, many of the practices established and honored within the ACA were not ones consortia originated by the member presidents could easily replicate.

who know me know that I am not stable—and I have no interest in being stable. If the ACA is going to stop growing, I am not interested in overseeing the maintenance of it." My frustration with many of the college presidents was that all they seemed to want to do was maintain their institutions, not make changes that would adapt them to the changing expectations of college students or the changing job market. Perhaps they did not want to try anything new until they were sure the new way would work better than the old way. They could not accept the idea that "perfection" can be the enemy of "good enough."[99] They would get so focused on the routine that they had no time for the experimental. From my experience, institutions that are not changing are dying. If a consortium is not experimenting and growing, it is getting closer to dissolving.[100]

The indications that the presidents wanted to hire someone who was less aggressive, less energetic, less persistent than I was came as a surprise to me. Then one of the presidents followed me out of the room and said, "You know what the problem is? These presidents never intended for your endowment to get bigger than theirs." It seems some of the presidents were delusional enough to think that the foundations, individuals, and federal agencies funding the ACA would fund their individual institutions if the ACA would just quit sending requests. The few ACA colleges that had received funding from Mellon and NSF and NEH before the ACA was established were still getting grants from those agencies at the same time the ACA

---

99. Bill Bowen was the first person to point out to me this problem of not getting a report done on time because I didn't think it was perfect. I had assumed he expected perfection.

100. I was frustrated by how reluctant some of the presidents were to put themselves into gatherings of representatives from colleges stronger than theirs were. Most ACA presidents were not risk takers.

was receiving funding. But most of the colleges had never gotten money from any of the foundations supporting the ACA. There was no reason to assume ACA colleges that had never been funded by large foundations or federal agencies should blame the ACA's success raising money for their inability to do so.

One reason this new push from some of the presidents surprised me was, at that time, fundraising had never been easier. No longer was I seeking new funding sources, I was receiving calls from funders seeking an introduction to the ACA. Foundations funding the ACA were sharing their interest with other foundations. Although the ACA was already doing what a foundation or individual wanted us to do with their money, the funders often had a project in mind that required modifications for it to fit within the scope of our existing administrative structure; I seldom had one that just wanted to give us money to expand or extend a program that was already operating successfully.[101] Yet, while most donors had their own ideas about how their money could best be used, most were willing to compromise.

The Ledford gift was an example: Colonel Ledford had wanted the ACA to give high school students in Harlan and surrounding counties scholarships so they could go to college, but the fact that we already had an administrative structure set up to give students in that region paid summer internships to help them stay in college was fine with him. He clearly did not want his money to go to establishing a new program that would require new employees and additional salaries. He just wanted his money to be used to help students from

---

101. Raising the endowment would be an exception to our established practices related to seeking funds for new projects. The endowment was intended to preserve programs already in place, such as fellowships.

his hometown and surrounding region to graduate from college. And that much we could promise.

Another example of how foundation officers were willing to compromise was the New York Community Trust. A new account established at the Trust was intended to encourage young people in KY and WV to major in medical fields. A program officer from the Trust called the Appalachian Regional Commission (ARC) and asked if the Federal Co-Chair could recommend an office to administer money designated for youth in WV and KY. The ARC response was "Call the ACA." When I responded that all we could do without adding additional staff was provide summer internships in medical facilities to students from ACA member colleges in WV and KY, the Trust representative thought that would fulfill their obligation to oversee the income from that trust—income which was expected to be about $100,000 annually. We promoted the new internships to ACA colleges in WV and KY with stipends that matched those we were giving students from all the member colleges for summer projects, such as those related to research with faculty and to community service projects.

Shortly after the call from the New York Community Trust, I took the newly appointed ACA vice president to New York with me to meet with staff at the Trust and talk about arrangements for awarding the funds available. In the middle of that conversation, this vice president interjected, "But if we can find another way to help these students with money from the Trust, such as . . ." I interrupted her and said, "No, the process for awarding the money that we have discussed is the only way the ACA can use money to fulfill obligations to donors." It was almost a certainty that the Trust staff didn't want to tell an association how they could work together, have that association agree that their staff could manage such a project, and then have someone say—but we don't really want to do that; let me tell you what we want to do.

Early in my career as a fundraiser, I had learned not to question the decision of a program officer even if I thought he or she was wrong: when I would explain what the ACA expected to do next, often the idea would be rejected. Then I would say, "I understand you don't think this idea is a good one; what strategy do you think we should pursue to strengthen our colleges?" John Stephenson had been quick to lead Claire List at Mellon to a way to help the Appalachian Center when she was not willing to pursue his original request.

My first experience of arguing with a foundation director taught me never to do that again. The director of a New York foundation invited me to come to New York to discuss how his foundation might help the ACP; he had heard about us from a college just outside the geographic region we served. The development director at that college had explained he thought it would be good for the ACA colleges to work more with their alumni for financial support. When I wrote the proposal to do that, I added to it helping the development or advancement officers generate support from multiple sources—not just alumni. The foundation director wrote back, saying he did not believe a college should ask people who had no prior affiliation with the college for money. I called him and pointed out that most of the graduates of the small colleges in our program were employed by non-profit agencies; many were ministers or schoolteachers. While they clearly appreciated the opportunities their colleges had provided, they were not financially able to send money to help the colleges. Such colleges often had to ask for financial support from people interested in the populations served, not just in the instruction provided. His response was that he "was not my private consultant." Then he called John Stephenson to complain about me. John called me and said, "That program officer doesn't like uppity Southern women."[102]

My last official contact with the ACA office came shortly after I retired and moved to NC: John Williams, who had been the ACA program contact for the Spencer Foundation, called and said that he was retired and wanted me to start a company and hire him to work with me. My response was, "You start the company and I'll work for you, but what is this company going to do?" He said that he had a number of friends who had held major positions in academic affairs, enrollment management, financial aid, student support, etc., at various colleges and were now retired and would like to work with the ACA colleges.[103] He had noticed that even the ACA colleges with strong presidents seldom had strong mid-level managers.

My response to Dr. Williams was, "But the colleges that need help cannot afford to pay us." John replied, "And that is why you are going to get a grant to fund our work." When I called Mellon, the program officer, Phil Lewis, indicated that the need for such a project was clear, and it was also clear that no one else was likely to be interested

---

102. I did go back to that foundation, but I never got a grant until that foundation officer retired and a new director was hired who was highly impressed with the work of the ACA and funded several grants for it.

103. John Chandler had told me that the person in charge of the grounds at Williams College (where he had been president) had called him and asked for help in developing a proposal for a sabbatical semester. Chandler had recommended that grounds keepers at ACA colleges should be contacted to see if any would like this horticulture expert to visit with them and make suggestions about beautifying the grounds at their colleges. Apparently, many of the participating colleges in the ACA welcomed the assistance; for years I heard it had been a major help to have expert advice regarding landscaping issues.

in fulfilling such a mission, but the grant would need to be awarded to the ACA. When I called the ACA and never was able to talk with Paul, the president, I asked the chief financial officer to tell the new president I needed to talk with him about this potential project. I did not hear from anyone at the ACA for a long time. When I called again, the answer I got from the CFO was, "If you bring five bags of gold up here to distribute across the ACA colleges, you won't be allowed to do so." It seemed clear that the ACA had moved past any interest in new projects that required fundraising.[104] The CFO told me that the only person Paul listened to was the chair of the ACA Governing Board, Dan Lunsford, president at Mars Hill College. "So," I said, "I'll talk to Dan." The CFO said, "It won't do any good; Dan thinks that if you hire someone you have to support him even if you don't agree with him." An article in *The Chronicle* refers to this practice as "back him or sack him."[105]

I am sure that a lot has changed in the ACA office. Obviously, fundraising has ceased to be a priority even though when I retired, roughly twenty funders were providing close to $5 million every year; and sustaining those relationships should have been relatively easy. But it does seem that the ACA board has fulfilled the vision for the ACA that the last strategic plan prior to my leaving indicated as a goal: they have "stabilized" the Association.

---

104. The chair of the search committee hiring the new ACA president had told me: "When you retire, we'll have to hire another woman, no man will work this hard at this level." Then he led the committee to hire a man.

105. The article in *The Chronicle*, by Michael Bills and Wallace Pond (Jan. 12, 2021), discusses the problems evolving from the belief by trustees that "they should unequivocally support the president until he or she becomes objectively and obviously unfit for the position."

Chapter 5

The Potential of Collaboration

I mentioned my plans to write this memoir to Lyle Roelofs, president at Berea College, and Pat McPherson, the vice president at Mellon who supported the ACA work throughout her ten years at the Foundation. Lyle indicated it could be helpful to new presidents at ACA colleges in understanding the development of the ACA; Pat suggested that as part of the memoir, I should comment on "how collaborations can be designed and ways they can fail—giving advice about how to maintain the important aspects while not preventing possibilities for development and appropriate change." Pat also mentioned that the memoir could provide valuable information for those seeking and those awarding grants.

Following are my thoughts about why the ACA was successful as an association serving the member colleges. Most consortia have a mission of sharing expertise and services across all the member institutions, and the success of such collaboration is hard to measure in concrete terms beyond considering the number of participants in the work of the consortium. The ACA served the member colleges by giving them access to resources from outside the member colleges, and it was easy to consider the amount of funding raised for the member colleges each year as an objective measure of success, as well as considering the number of participants in each opportunity provided. As Tish Emerson, when she was the ACA program officer at Mellon, indicated: funding from such a distinguished foundation as Mellon provides credibility that leads other funders to endorse the colleges benefiting from the largesse of The Andrew W. Mellon Foundation. Also, the colleges that took advantage of ACA benefits could list major foundations and federal agencies that supported their faculty and students. Such endorsements could be beneficial in raising the status of a college in the eyes of other donors and potential students and faculty.

Other regional consortia, such as the Associated Colleges of the South (ACS), the Great Lakes Colleges Association (GLCA), and the Associated Colleges of the Midwest (ACM), are different from the ACA in that the member institutions are wealthy compared to most in the ACA. They are not so dependent on outside funding as most of the ACA colleges are. When I spoke to a group of presidents from the ACM and the GLCA, hosted by Mellon, one of the Mellon program officers said, "If you take Berea and Sewanee out of the ACA, any college in this room will have an endowment larger than all the other ACA colleges put together." One ACA president moved to a college in the Associated Colleges of the Midwest. When I learned that he was paying about $40,000 in dues to the ACM, I called to tell him I remembered when he complained about his ACA dues of about $4,000. He said that the college he served in the ACM could better afford the $40,000 dues than the ACA college could afford the $4,000 dues.

The leaders at most of these financially stable institutions are not intimidated by new practices, new technologies, or new content. They are, as the president at Centre College once told me, "risk takers" while few ACA colleges can afford to be very bold in trying new approaches or taking major risks. But the leaders of those associations, no doubt, have their own theories about what has kept their consortia strong. A part of the success of all our histories has been the growing interest of funding agencies in supporting consortia. Sustaining that interest has required each consortium to be able to demonstrate success.

Following is a list of the benefits the ACA provided during its first twenty-five years of operating; the ones with an asterisk are endowed.

For faculty:

- We gave sabbaticals to faculty at colleges that did not have sabbaticals and extra time for research to those who did have sabbaticals.*

- We sent the faculty to nationally and internationally sponsored seminars.*

- We gave science faculty access to labs and equipment and supplies for research they could not conduct on their own campuses.*

- We provided (through UK) a repair service for equipment important in science instruction.

- We took faculty teaching in the arts to Pittsburgh to have experiences with and learn from performing arts organizations there, and we brought Pittsburgh Opera interns to ACA campuses to demonstrate the beauty and power of opera.

- We helped faculty interested in entrepreneurship develop courses, a unique opportunity since fellowship funds were not to be used for course development.

- We funded faculty interested in environmental science to conduct research with the Appalachian Labs in Frostburg, Maryland, part of the University of Maryland System.

For faculty and students:

- We gave faculty and students money to work with each other on research topics.*

- We gave faculty and students money to participate in service-learning projects.

- We gave faculty and students opportunities to travel and study abroad and, in some cases, to participate in Salzburg Seminars.

- We gave ACA colleges money so their faculty and students could work with local community leaders to help with regional economic development.

- We provided workshops for faculty on how to use technology in teaching and trained their students to help with the technical features of the new pedagogies.

For students:

- We gave students NOYCE and C-STEM scholarships from NSF which not only supported their educations but also helped with applications they might make to graduate programs and jobs.

- We gave students opportunities to have internships in medical fields.

- We hosted the annual weekend Summit and the summer week-long Teaching Institute to provide time for ACA discipline groups to work together and to learn from experts in their fields.*

For libraries:

- We created the Digital Library of Appalachia and put millions of digitally enhanced publications on ACA campuses, and we provided training for librarians on the latest techniques for incorporating online materials into class content so they could teach the faculty. *

- We made it possible for all ACA colleges to access JSTOR and Artstor.*

Other:

- We conducted research to determine the outcomes of students at ACA colleges compared to outcomes for students at public regional universities and trained faculty to do similar research studies.

- We created an alliance of the graduate deans at the major research universities in the region who assisted with reviewing fellowship applications, waived out-of-state tuition for ACA faculty in their graduate programs, provided access to their resources and facilities for training or ACA workshops, and added spaces in their grant requests for ACA faculty to participate with their faculty.

Obviously, not every faculty member from every ACA college was interested in all these opportunities, but with about 3,000 faculty across the thirty-five or so colleges, there were always some faculty interested in each. Also, the ACA never set out to do so much; it was intended to provide support to faculty working to upgrade their academic credentials and/or improve their expertise in the fields they taught. The inclusion of the multiple projects that took place over the twenty-five years I led the Association could be attributed to ideas faculty, academic deans, presidents, and potential funders identified to help the faculty and students at the member colleges. The ACA simply wrote the proposals for the grants that made those ideas possible.

We did not provide all the programs mentioned at one time, but we did many of them all the time. There were multiple opportunities that were available only for a day or so—such as the convening of science faculty to meet with representatives from NSF to determine the needs of the ACA faculty that NSF might help address. But the benefits listed above lasted at least a year and, in most cases, three years or longer. Almost half of the opportunities for students and faculty are endowed, and with the support of the multiple major foundations that had provided support to the ACA for as long as twenty-five years, there were reasons, at the time I retired, to expect that contributions to the endowments and for other projects would continue for many more years.

Building and Sustaining a Successful Consortium

1. The first element critical to building any successful venture *is having a worthy mission and a vision of how to fulfill it.* ACA's mission was to strengthen private colleges in central Appalachia by bringing benefits to the colleges from outside those colleges—

benefits that few of the colleges could afford or attract by themselves but would give those at the colleges access to resources that would enhance their educational experiences.[105]

2. After having a worthy mission and a commitment to honor promises made, *having financial support* is a critical element for the success of a consortium or association. We could have done little if we had not had generous financial support from multiple funders. Typically, several million dollars a year resulted from the submission of perhaps a dozen requests for support as well as from funders who contacted the ACA offering help. My goal was to have at least three proposals pending and at least five more in preparation. Even I find it amazing how easy it was to interest potential funders in a program where thirty-five or so colleges, most with about 1,000 to 1,500 residential students from disadvantaged backgrounds, could be helped with one major contribution. And I think I made it clear that we were willing to work with the potential funding agencies to help them meet their goals while they were helping us meet ours.

3. To maintain funding for a successful venture *accountability is important*. We held the attention of major funders and attracted the attention of others by being very transparent; there were not many questions that could not be answered by looking at our website. Sources of funding, financial reports, individuals, and projects supported were covered on that site.

---

105. While it may be safe to assume that this original mission would continue to be the driving force behind the growth of the association, it may be unrealistic for me to make that assumption a dozen years after I left the association; therefore, the use of past tense in referring to that mission.

One foundation officer said we "buried" our funders in reports, often letting them know even after their funding had ended how the project(s) they had funded were still benefiting those at the colleges. The major funders of the endowment received reports every year that I was president listing the faculty and students who had benefited from their generosity—even if that generosity had occurred years earlier. When we published our first annual report a couple of years after I became director of the Appalachian College Program, one of our first funders who, it seems, had not thought about us since approving our early application, called to tell me how impressed he was by our growing success. Then we remained in touch throughout my term at UK and my tenure with the ACA in Berea.

4. *Having name recognition* may not be critical to successful fundraising, but it certainly helped. When I started developing proposals for funding and talking with potential funders, I called Mike Zoob, who led the fundraising of the national Elderhostel office when it was becoming a registered independent, not-for-profit organization. He had raised money from foundations like Kellogg and ARCO, and I thought I needed his advice. His response was that raising money for Elderhostel was difficult because he had to explain to potential donors what Elderhostel was in a way that built confidence that it was a secure organization and not just some social movement. Raising money for a program based at UK would be easy because the university was already known to be sustainable. He was right. When I mentioned the Appalachian College Program, there was seldom a reaction until I added "based at the University of Kentucky." Other consortia might be able to

get a positive reaction by naming a couple of the best known of their participating colleges or universities. After a dozen years at UK, the ACA itself had name recognition.

5. Another helpful, if not essential, characteristic of having a successful consortium or association *is having a target population that can respond to opportunities without a complicated, bureaucratic process to gain permission to respond*. When John Stephenson gained approval for funding faculty at small private colleges, he didn't stipulate an application process that required multiple levels of approval from the applicant's college administrators. Applications called for a letter of support from the applicant's academic dean, but those letters usually seemed little more than a form letter of approval that could apply to almost any faculty member at almost any college. Fortunately, John started the Appalachian College Program to serve those he knew needed to be served, and he didn't require any strong endorsement from anyone above the applicant on his/her home campus.

John didn't initially contact the presidents of the colleges; he didn't ask permission from the academic deans; he didn't even have permission from UK academic divisions to negotiate with Claire List at Mellon. He worked out an agreement that both the foundation and he could comfortably endorse as promising to address both the foundation's goals and his goals as director of the Appalachian Center at UK. Having been a faculty member at an ACA college (Lees-McRae), he understood the need of many faculty for opportunities that let them leave the confines of their small college and conduct research where there were major resources in their disciplines, have content-based discussions with multiple faculty knowledgeable in their disciplines, and enjoy relaxing in a community where there were numerous institutions of cultural or historical interest, such as theatres and museums. John might have even realized that some academic deans would not promote opportunities which would take faculty away from their campus assignments for a semester or a year, and that he would need to encourage the early participants to help generate interest in fellowships and travel grants.

6. To sustain a consortium, *it is important that the institutional leaders are willing to admit they can benefit from working with other colleges—or at least willing to allow their faculty and other administrators to do so.* It is extremely helpful if the participating parties understand that helping another college does not weaken theirs, that cooperation is more beneficial than competition, and that when they agree to collaborate, they and others at their colleges should look out for each other and give priority to the other members of the collaborative. For example, when a student indicates plans to leave a college or university, student affairs officials should recommend to that student that he or she consider other colleges in the ACA. When a president is asked to nominate another president for special recognition, he should nominate one from the consortium—especially if there are thirty or more from which to choose.[106] The presidents in the ACA too often didn't seem

---

106. I use these two examples because they had happened: one president told me he realized he should have been referring those dropping out of his college because its wasn't "religious enough" to some of the other ACA colleges, and I witnessed an award ceremony where none of the ACA college presidents had nominated another ACA president.

willing to recommend an ACA program even if they publicly praised it. Shortly before I retired, at a meeting of the ACA presidents, the answer to one question made clear how most, if not all, of the presidents felt about the ACA. The question was, "If there was a storm that destroyed multiple buildings on one of the member campuses, would the rest of the colleges come together to help that college recover?" After a long silence, the answer was, "We would come if Alice called and told us helping was a priority for the ACA." The observation was that while each president was, at least to some degree, committed to the ACA, they were not committed to each other.[107] One might have thought that as presidents of Christian liberal arts colleges, they would have cared about each other more than it seems they did.

7. *Another element critical to the success of a consortium is the willingness of presidents of the member colleges to have a spirit of adventure, a willingness to take at least small risks.* What too often surprised me was the reluctance of presidents to involve their institutions in a new ACA venture—even when it wasn't going to cost the college anything. For example, when Spencer and Mellon offered funding for a study to compare the success of graduates from ACA private colleges to those from public regional universities in one of the states served, only about a dozen of the member colleges were interested

---

107. When I asked why president were so reluctant to collaborate, one consortia director wrote to me that presidents don't want to collaborate because of their insecurity. "They know they are not really in 'command' of their own institution, but never want to admit it. Certainly not to their board, or their faculty, or their alleged colleagues." It is a shame that more presidents of struggling colleges don't seem to want to learn from their more successful colleagues.

in participating. One president was bold enough to admit that he was afraid the results of the study would expose the weaknesses of the small Appalachian private colleges. Why did he not think that studying ACA colleges might reveal the strengths of the colleges? A major benefit to participation in the study was that ACT (with a connection to the primary researcher at the University of Iowa) could find addresses the college did not have for some of its alumni. At another time, an academic dean told me he did not want data about his students compared with similar data about students from other colleges; he just wanted his faculty and staff to make comparisons between current and past data from his college.[108] Events for faculty were usually what was most successful; faculty from every college were hungry for opportunities to travel, do research, and involve their students in research. They were much less cautious about participating in a new adventure than the presidents and academic deans were.

8. *Having an expanding basis of financial support is important to sustaining a collaborative or association of colleges.* The critical element for the ACA's success was the generosity of The Andrew W. Mellon Foundation. That support gave the ACA a presence in the world of non-profit funding that enabled me to get through the door of many other foundations. Many of the funders of the ACA were attracted to the Association because they respected

---

108. When Johanna Brownell was editing a draft of this memoir, her comment at this point was, "This is problematic on so many levels; remaining so insular can ultimately cost a college or university in both funding and students. It would be great if you could discuss it." Unfortunately, I often marveled at how many presidents wanted to surround their colleges in secrecy—hardly a way to attract students. I could never understand why presidents were so insular, so I certainly cannot explain their reason for being so.

Mellon's judgment. The Pew Charitable Trusts was the second major foundation to fund the predecessor of the ACA—the ACP. I loved hearing Mellon and Pew representatives argue about who had given money to the ACA first and who had given more. While some of the ACA presidents made clear their concern that the ACA was not addressing their concerns, it was unrealistic to expect that outside funding could be secured for the personal preferences of a small subset of the member colleges. To address specific concerns of specific colleges (such as wanting help encouraging local high school students to attend their colleges), it should be clear to members that as benefits increase, dues may need to increase. The ACA was lucky enough to keep finding the funds to continuously increase opportunities available, but when the presidents want to have the major voice in determining priorities for their consortia, they need to realize the importance of increasing their dues to support their ideas. The member colleges should expect to be a part of expanding the financial support of their association.

9. Perhaps one thing that has made the ACA sustainable *is having an endowment to which every college contributed financially.* Nothing will keep a college president's attention like monitoring where his/her money went—and what it has purchased that he/she values. When the ACA started raising the endowment that would sustain at least the fellowships in the humanities, and it seemed NEH was going to provide a million dollars and Mellon would match it with three million, I learned from a foundation that once the ACA itself raised another million, that foundation would provide an additional million. The person who made this offer was about to retire, so I called the

Executive Committee and said the only way I knew to raise that million within the next couple of months was for each college to give the ACA $30,000 for the endowment.

With only a couple of exceptions, each college quickly sent a check to the ACA. The exceptions later made their contributions. That contribution entitled each college to access the endowment income for fellowships for the faculty. But it also has, I suspect, kept presidents from leaving the ACA and access to the opportunities their colleges helped fund. Those $30,000 contributions are not refundable, and neither is the interest that has accumulated. On the other hand, the $30,000 required contribution, plus interest earned since the endowment was established, are now requirements for admission to the ACA, beyond the other requirements (location in central Appalachia, accreditation by a regional accreditor, and commitment to the region). It is unlikely any private college not already a member of the ACA but eligible for membership will be able to meet this new requirement for a donation to the endowment.

The new president at the University of the South (Sewanee) at the time I was asking for $30,000 from each college seemed to have some reservations about making that contribution. A friend there suggested I come to Sewanee so she could host a lunch for the new president and faculty who had benefited from ACA fellowships. At the lunch, each faculty member spoke about what he or she had been able to accomplish with funding from the ACA. After a while, the president turned to me and asked if Mellon knew I was funding Sewanee.

I was surprised by the question but answered, "Of course they do; you're in our annual reports."

"If I leave this table and call Bill Bowen and ask him why Mellon funds the ACA and why faculty from Sewanee are eligible when we clearly do not need the money as much as other ACA colleges, what will he say."

My response was: "He'll say, 'We fund the ACA to strengthen private colleges in Appalachia, and you do not strengthen the weak by isolating them from the strong.'" The president nodded; and a few days later, a check from Sewanee arrived at the ACA.

One other college was delinquent in sending $30,000 for the endowment, but it was a college where the academic dean had just been named president, and I assumed the transition had slowed the response to the request from the ACA. When I attended his inauguration, I followed him around the campus until I could catch him by himself. When he told me that he had to think about whether his college should pay the $30,000, I pointed out to him that all the other college presidents in the ACA had already thought about it, and they had all decided to send the ACA a check. Shortly thereafter, a check from that college arrived at the ACA.[109]

One of the colleges which did not have $30,000 in the budget that could be sent to the ACA withdrew $30,000 from their endowment, rationalizing that the money would still be in an endowment that would benefit the institution.

---

109. This experience reminds me of one where one ACA president told another, "You may as well say, 'Yes,' when Alice asks you to do something because she is not going to leave you alone until you do." Of course, some presidents praised my persistence; others complimented my ability to graciously accept a negative response.

10. *Having "partner or affiliated institutions" helps assure credibility.* I suspect that the affiliation of the six major research universities in the five states of the ACA that kept graduate deans at those universities involved in evaluating the fellowship applications has also helped sustain the consortium. I know that at least some of the ACA college presidents were pleased by the recognition their faculty received from those affiliations and by the fact that, in some cases, the graduate deans and their staff provided special services for the ACA colleges, such as providing faculty from the universities to serve as outside examiners for students graduating with honors from the ACA college. In other cases, faculty brought back to their private college equipment that was no longer in use at one of the major universities. One faculty member from a TN college returned to his campus with a travel trailer to use on geological field trips. I know that this affiliation has provided the assurance that fellowships funded will be awarded for appropriate academic research, not because a dean needs one of the faculty members to have a terminal degree for the college to maintain accreditation in a field (such as business), and that assurance has meant that those approached for funding could give without concern for the quality of the research or graduate study to be funded.

11. *Having people able and willing to provide advice for new directors.* There is now an association of consortia directors – the Association of Collaborative Leadership (ACL)—that has over fifty committed consortia directors as members. The increase in resources available to help those trying to develop

consortia, or at least a collaborative program, bodes well for the sustainability of these efforts.

12. Perhaps a critical element to assuring the success of a consortium is *having a governing board that can see the whole body instead of the individual members.* As Franklin Patterson says in his book *Colleges in Consort*,[110] "Even in the best of these [consortia], institutional autonomy and self-interest remain the predominant pattern, and cooperative endeavors appear thin" (p. 28). Patterson was the first president of Hampshire College, an institution formed by a group of other colleges. He was well versed in the problems associated with trying to get multiple independent colleges to perform as one, at least in some aspects of their operations.

A point in Patterson's book that is all too true from my perspective is that presidents "are not directly enough concerned with securing the benefits of the consortium or maintaining and developing its quality to be its appropriate governors . . . ." He believed that there is "no reason why the board-of-presidents model of governance for service consortia should exist" (p. 47). He recommended that consortia should be "independent of the institutions served, governed by those with a direct commitment to its success in serving colleges . . . economically and with high educational quality." "A strong executive would be in charge" and could focus on the quality and financial feasibility of services offered without being preoccupied with "keeping his band of institutional barons happy" (p. 48).

---

110. San Francisco: Jossey-Bass, 1974.

This philosophy of governance is like that in business which says that the governors of an organization should not be the beneficiaries of the services of that organization. It can be hard to be objective if you are to benefit personally from a decision made by the governing board on which you serve.

Patterson thought that consortia could best be governed by people external to the members of the consortia, although he did spend a little time considering the idea of having a trustee from each member of a consortium serve as the governing board (p. 53). The advantages of such a board include (1) the fact that trustees often have more time to devote to consortia than presidents; (2) trustees can have a more detached perspective than the presidents; (3) since trustees are the agents responsible for the long-term interests of a college, they would be better prepared to think about the long-term stability of the consortium than a group of presidents are likely to be. Too many presidents have to worry about the short-term stability of their colleges.

While I know of no consortia governed by trustees of the member colleges, I would like to know the reaction of presidents to that idea. The presidents of ACA colleges never wanted their trustees involved in any program that involved cross-campus collaboration; they did not want their trustees in a position to compare the various colleges' progress, success, or failures across multiple institutions that were often remarkably similar. But the mission of a consortium—be it providing services or encouraging cooperation—could, according to Patterson, determine whether trustees would be the better governors (p. 62).[111]

I often thought that the ACA Advisory Council would have better served as the board for the Association than the presidents did. As Beth Baxter said in the strategic plan that created that Council, the Association needs leaders who can be objective about what is the greatest benefit for the most colleges. It was clear to me in working with the dozen or so on the Advisory Council that their collective vision for the ACA was much clearer than that of the thirty-five plus presidents.

13. Patterson goes so far as to say that there is no sign that cooperation is natural or evolutionary. For example, if faculty are to be involved in cooperating in a significant way, the consortium must accomplish that feature by either seduction or coercion. "Seduction is considered by most consortia as the more appealing route, although, as a general rule, it has thus far failed" (p. 55). He suggests that to encourage cooperation by the faculty, representative faculty must be involved in the decision-making and operating aspects of the association and must be flattered throughout their participation. One of my great mistakes was, I think now, never having an active advisory committee of faculty from across the member colleges.

At the time Patterson was writing, he discussed how the Five Colleges, Inc. had an office independent of any member institution, but each college had someone who worked for that

---

111. Elizabeth Hayford, who co-authored a book about trusteeship with me, reminded me about how difficult it is to get strong individuals, with relevant experience and expertise, to serve as trustees at small, struggling colleges. It might also, she told me, be hard to get exceptional trustees to serve on the boards of consortia. However, some trustees might find governing a consortium that can impact multiple colleges more appealing than governing just one college.

association. There was one college in the ACA that had at least one period of time where it was exceeding all the other member colleges in getting fellowships and other awards from the ACA. When I questioned their success, I learned that when the head of development at the college retired, everyone seemed to expect that the person who had served for a long time as the second-in-command in the development office would have been named the director. When the president chose an outside person for the position and realized he had alienated many of the faculty and staff of the college by that decision, he asked the woman rejected to serve as the person in charge of helping faculty find grant funding. She became masterful at identifying good faculty with good projects for the ACA. It is hard to imagine how successful the ACA would have been with one employee from each member college working with the Association.

It is important to remember that the primary beneficiaries of the work of the ACA were expected to be faculty and students. It was by giving faculty opportunities to enhance their expertise and students opportunities to enrich their educational experiences that the ACA and the funders believed would strengthen the member colleges. While we occasionally gathered groups of financial officers or IT staff or marketing employees, it was the faculty whom we targeted when we were raising money. I believed that it was faculty who attracted students to the colleges, kept them enrolled, and saw them through to graduation. When alumni give to their alma maters, it is usually because they remember one or more faculty members who gave them the skills they needed to be successful. It is interesting that most of our work with students was initiated by NSF, the Ledford Foundation, and the

New York Community Trust. Various foundations and federal agencies clearly had priorities that guided our requests to them.

It would have been interesting, if someone had offered to fund a priority of the presidents, if the presidents could have agreed on one thing that outside funding would do to enhance the experiences students and faculty could have on each campus. A Mellon program officer once asked me if bringing all the presidents to New York to talk about the benefits women in administration bring to a college would result in the presidents returning to their campuses to hire more women deans—or at least more women chairs. I didn't think that such an experience would impact more than a couple of the presidents. Another time, a foundation asked if they gave one of the ACA colleges a million dollars to spend the next couple of years closing, would that college close or would it use the million and then claim reasons not to close. I had lied only once to a major contributor.[112] I would not lie this time. Neither encouraging women to have major roles in the administration of their colleges nor closing were priorities for many of the ACA college presidents.

Faculty who received fellowships in the early years of the Appalachian College Program would return to their campuses with praise for the experience; eventually enough faculty had received fellowships that their enthusiasm encouraged their deans to endorse the opportunities. The deans saw the ACA as a way to provide faculty support and to meet and commiserate with others in positions like theirs. Many of the deans told their presidents about the opportunities being provided by

---

112. When NSF asked me if I thought UK would continue funding the repair van for science faculty if NSF provided funding for a second three-year cycle, I said "Yes." I had just left UK, and many there were not pleased I had left. I couldn't make myself hurt the University by saying it was not likely UK would cover the costs to help the ACA colleges keep their scientific equipment up and running.

a program at UK. Thus, when the ACA was formed and dues were set, most of the presidents were willing to join; they encouraged other of the ACA colleges' presidents. For presidents who remained reluctant to pay dues to this new association, the librarians were able to point to savings that could be realized with access to the Central Library. The librarians, in fact, became the most vocal group supporting the opportunities provided.

With thirty-five or so colleges and 50,000 or so students,[113] it was easy to point out to donors how many faculty and students are still denied opportunities that would improve their experiences in higher education and their chances of success in the world. The mission of strengthening private higher education in central Appalachia was an easy one to support. Who could be opposed to helping those who had endured multiple disadvantages in life find their way out of poverty through educational institutions with exceptional faculty and multiple supplemental opportunities?

And it was all the colleges as a group that made it possible to bring resources to the individual colleges. Only a couple of the member colleges were large enough or wealthy enough to bring such resources to their campuses; most were too small and too poor to attract such benefits. As I mentioned earlier, NSF representatives asked the ACA to send proposals for multiple, if not all, of the colleges, because so many of the member colleges were not strong enough to be competitive in a national arena—an arena that might be a federal agency or a major foundation. Repeatedly, I heard from faculty that friends of theirs in

---

113. The current ACA website indicates that there are 77,000 students at the member colleges now; the number of those students taking only courses online is not indicated.

much larger and wealthier colleges or universities were jealous of all the opportunities ACA faculty could access. Still, we never reached the 40,000 feet Tish Emerson mentioned at the tenth-anniversary celebration of the ACA; we never got beyond 30,000 feet even though Mellon, with Tish's lead, seemed prepared to help us go higher.[114]

At a national meeting of consortia directors shortly before I retired, I was asked to speak about fundraising for a consortium (since I had raised over $40 million at that time). I talked about how to identify and approach potential donors and how to shape a proposal to meet the requirements for funding, which often requires revisions to accommodate priorities of the funder as well as the needs of the consortium.

After my presentation, one of the consortia directors said, "But I think my job is to fulfill the vision of my presidents for our consortium; you fulfilled your vision." My response was, "If the presidents of the ACA colleges had a vision for the ACA, I would have been happy to try to fulfill it; the problem with thirty-five or so college presidents is that there is a lot of variation in their visions; what most want is money given to them for the needs of their individual campuses, not money given to the ACA to meet the needs of the colleges as a group—especially when the needs identified that are clearly fundable usually reflect the needs of faculty and/or students, not the buildings the presidents typically want.

Another problem with having a board of thirty-five college presidents is that most of the presidents assumed the executive committee of presidents would represent what all the presidents wanted. The fact was that not all the presidents ever wanted what I thought I could

---

114. Tish did write to me in an email (Jan. 13, 2021) to point out that "without Bill Bowen's encouragement and willingness" to give her "space to try new things, the story would have been very different."

find a foundation or other agency to fund. The priorities for the ACA depended on who was on the executive committee at any one time. The composition of that committee required, for some reason, that every president have a chance to serve on it. Thus, at some point, the presidents who had not served were from among the most financially fragile of the colleges. Their priorities were not the priorities of the more financially secure campuses.

It was important that I could *honor the promises made* to funders; it was not the presidents who were responsible for seeing that the day-to-day operations of the ACA were steps to fulfilling promises made. As I have indicated, I quickly grew comfortable with the vision of the staff at the foundations supporting the ACA. Most employees at major foundations have experiences exploring new approaches to education and seeing what has worked well. Their advice always seemed wise to me; the advice of the presidents, not so much.

When several presidents mentioned the need for opportunities for their faculty and students to study abroad, they wrote a proposal for funding their plan. When that plan was rejected by potential funders, one of the retired college presidents, Fred Mullinax, went to the Berger Foundation and returned with a grant to fund international study for faculty and students at ACA colleges. I tried to be sure that the ACA was fulfilling the vision of Berger for the use of its money—not the vision the group of ACA presidents had documented. While I don't remember what was different about the proposal of the ACA group of presidents and the proposal that Berger funded, I suspect that when Fred met with the head of the Berger Foundation, there were various compromises that were involved in finalizing a significant grant proposal for students and faculty to travel and study abroad. Later,

Christian A. Johnson Endeavor Fund extended the opportunities for international studies and experiences.[115]

Each funding source had its own vision of what the ACA should be doing, and it was important that once the ACA accepted funding from that source, the vision of the source was incorporated into the goals of the Association. The ACA did not take money under one pretense and use it for another. Promises I made were promises kept—at least until it was evident that I had tried to fulfill the promises made but had to admit that obstacles to fulfilling those promises were likely to prevent success. As Martha Perry, the program officer from one of the major funders of the ACA, said at my retirement dinner: "You could trust Alice to tell you the truth; if something was not working, she would tell you that. Many people we fund think we only want to hear about all the good being accomplished, not about all the problems they are encountering."

Closing a Consortium

Patterson offered one answer to Pat McPherson's question about why consortia fail: the consortia were composed primarily of only a few colleges with little financial strength, and when one or

---

115. For one annual meeting, the president of the CAJ Fund called and recommended a presenter for the upcoming annual meeting. She added that if that person heard from the ACA presidents that there was a need that could be addressed collectively by at least some, if not all, of the colleges, CAJ might fund a project to address that need. At the meeting, most of the presidents were not just unreceptive to the speaker, they were almost rude (talking among themselves during the presentation, sending me messages to get her to end her presentation). On the ride to dinner that night, as I was driving the speaker and the Mellon representative attending the meeting to dinner, I overheard the Mellon person apologizing to the speaker for the behavior of the presidents. Perhaps if I had mentioned the connection of the speaker to the CAJ fund, the presidents would have paid more attention.

two colleges wanted to leave the consortium, there were too few remaining members to sustain the collaboration. Of course, if the member colleges are among the wealthier ones in the nation, the smaller group can probably increase dues enough to sustain the consortium. But Patterson was more familiar with "colleges with little financial strength"—the kind of colleges that make up the majority of those in the ACA. What the ACA has that not many consortia have is a compelling mission that has attracted enough money to build a substantial endowment: helping faculty working with students from disadvantaged regions by giving them educational experiences that can lead to a life of purposeful work and integrity. This mission has a natural appeal to the compassion and charity of us all—and certainly to those funding worthwhile programs.

Patterson lists roughly eighty-five consortia in his book; it would be interesting to study how many of those are still in existence and how many new ones have been formed since 1974 and what has determined longevity and what has encouraged the creation of new associations for collaboration. There are a lot of purposes for consortia, and those are usually dependent on whether the member colleges are located near to each one, where travel between the institutions is easy (such as the Boston Consortium), or where the colleges are located across multiple states (such as the Appalachian College Association, the Great Lakes Colleges Association, the Associated Colleges of the South, and the Associated Colleges of the Midwest). It seems obvious that if the benefits prove irrelevant to most of the campus populations or if the benefits provided do not seem worth the membership fees charged, the consortium will not survive. Charts reflecting money invested and the financial value gained, I suspect, have kept some colleges in the ACA.

The consortia I knew that have closed did so for various reasons. In some cases, it was an unclear mission: starting a consortium with the expectation of eventually finding a reason for the consortium to exist. Or it was unrealistic expectations that enticed colleges to join the consortium but soon leave when promises made were not kept—or were not kept quickly enough. Some increased the membership too quickly and could not give each of the member colleges enough attention. A consortium in Texas that had member colleges and member corporations found the two groups were not so compatible. Another reason for closing a consortium in Texas was the spending of money for an expensive headquarters building when, it seems, the only one who thought that was an essential element for the consortium was the consortium director.

As I mentioned in the section about the Ledford lawsuit, when Josephson of the Attorney General's office asked about the difference between the foundations I was used to working with (such as Mellon, Exxon, McCune, etc.) and the Ledford Foundation, I said, "Greed." I suspect this is a reason some consortia fail. From eighty-five consortia in 1974 to roughly fifty today,[116] incompetence is probably less to blame than greed in organizations where too few layers of oversight are present to assure accuracy in financial reports. There are too few laws governing financial oversight for most nonprofit organizations and far too little transparency that could expose unethical or even illegal transactions or practices.

Patterson asserts that in the 1970s foundations and federal funders were too parsimonious in responding to consortia when they asked

---

116. The number eighty-five is based on those listed by Patterson; the number fifty is based on membership in the ACL; surely, there are additional consortia that do not belong to the ACL. There does not seem to be a way to determine an accurate count of consortia operating today. An accreditation or licensing agency might provide a good approximation.

for help and therefore failed to encourage consortia to move forward with new models of collaboration. He complains about "the baggage of institutional autonomy" which hinders the pace of leadership in collaboration. His solution to enhancing interest and speeding development is "money wisely invested by foundations" (p. 122). The ACA has certainly had that.

Building the ACA from the bottom up and finding an ever-increasing number of funders has helped to create a sustainable organization. But the fact that an organization is sustainable doesn't mean that it will be sustained. The results of the coronavirus will certainly stress the financial stability of many colleges, leading some to reduce expenditures, and some reductions are likely to include not paying dues to consortia.

My Dream Consortium

If I were starting a consortium of private colleges today, the critical element would be funding from a foundation or transformational donor for at least three years with the member colleges agreeing to provide an annual fee based on some aspects of their data (enrollment, expenditures, number of faculty, etc.) and the cost of maintaining a central office. The important element would be trustees who have no previous affiliation with any of the colleges involved but significant experience in working with private colleges and a concern for the region where member colleges are located. I would work to involve the members not only with strengths they each could offer to the others, but also with resources and expertise from outside the network of member colleges.

The experiences ACA faculty had with faculty from the affiliated research universities and with those at national conferences clearly had a strong impact on all those involved. I think that having a board that is independent of any of the colleges would help assure that priority for projects (which to maintain, which to "sunset," and which to introduce) would not be determined by which of the college presidents are on the Executive Committee and could sway decisions to those that best meet the needs of their colleges with little regard for the needs of most of the colleges.

In addition to having a Presidents' Council and a Deans' Council, I would have a Faculty Council. The Faculty Council would be comprised of two professors from each member college—one from a humanities division and another from a science division. Each council would meet independently to make recommendations that could then be presented to the board of independent advisors, none with strong connections to any college in the consortium. I would take advantage of lessons learned late in my terms at the ACA, such as making efforts to get young faculty involved in ACA opportunities rather than allowing the program to become one where the benefits are monopolized by tenured faculty. I would insist on transparency in the operations of the consortium, publicizing annual budgets, awards made, services offered, etc.—in short, documenting benefits as well as costs for each college.

Conclusion

I hope I have made it clear that leading the ACA or its precursor programs from 1983 until 2008, despite the challenges I had to face to keep it thriving, was the best job I could imagine. Faculty appreciated me because I brought them opportunities that would probably never have been available to them without the ACA; students (who probably didn't have a clue who I was) had experiences that could give them a step up when applying to graduate school or for a job after college; academic deans relished the opportunities the ACA provided for them to get together; and presidents tolerated the ACA because it provided faculty development opportunities they either had no interest in or no funding to provide; they even came to appreciate it when their librarians could show them the savings being realized.

The best part was that people and organizations could see the benefits their contributions to the ACA were providing to thousands of faculty and tens of thousands of students. I loved the praise I received from people whose status would have made it impossible for me to meet them without the ACA. Bill Bowen always enclosed a handwritten note with each check sent to the ACA indicating how pleased he was to be able to help our worthwhile efforts. Bert Ifill at Mellon said, "You could do anything anywhere and make more money than you're making here, but you are truly committed to the cause of the program";[116] Ilene Mack at Hearst said I was one of the few people she knew who was as comfortable in New York meeting with the head of a foundation as I was in Appalachia meeting with a cook at one of the poorest colleges in the nation.

The retirement dinner was a wonderful celebration for me. Bill Bowen attended, as well as Barbara Robinson, Tish Emerson, Duncan McBride from NSF, Martha Perry from McCune, and many others who had made the ACA not just possible but extremely successful. The speeches made in my honor were so flattering I suspect my family who attended thought I had written them myself. Jean Ritchie and Doug Orr and his wife provided the music, and the evening ended to the sound of "Amazing Grace."

I certainly cannot say, as a colleague suggested, that I have "saved a region"; I haven't even saved a college. But like all those college teachers across central Appalachia, I do believe that I have made a lot of lives a little better.

---

116. For a minute, I was tempted to ask where these other opportunities were.

Acknowledgements

When I first started thinking about the people who helped me with this memoir, I realized that I was listing not just those who helped with this memoir, but also those who had helped build and sustain the ACA during the time I led the Association. That list was long and full of distinguished higher education leaders, and there would have been no ACA without their exceptional advice and hard work. They all deserve more praise than I can offer here, so I have limited myself to giving a few special recognitions:

Bill Bowen, who died in 2016, repeatedly "fixed" problems for me: he gave emergency funds when the ACA endowment was too young to produce enough; he found pro bono lawyers when there was a lawsuit; he even stayed in touch with me after I retired, keeping me involved in the life of small private colleges even after I left the ACA. There are many times when I wish I could talk with him, but I read his books and ask myself: "What would Bill do?" or "What would Bill say?" I think he would have encouraged this memoir. It is remarkable how the memory of someone can continue to provide inspiration for many years after he or she is no longer in your life.

Alice (Tish) Emerson was my contact person at Mellon for most of the time I was leading the UK program and the ACA. She is mentioned multiple times in this memoir. She was the most creative person I ever worked with; she led me through the implementation of her ideas for the ACA—not one of which I would have been able to envision without her: (1) she moved the ACA to projects focusing on technology at an appropriate time; (2) she nurtured the growth of the Central Library; and (3) she was the one who suggested the creation of the endowment and instructed me to be sure to make it clear that no changes could be made in that agreement without approval from the contributors.[117] She knew the world of higher education and watched it carefully as innovations came fast and furiously between roughly 1991 and 2002. Without those frequent calls from Tish, the ACA would have been but a shadow of itself when I retired.

Others who deserve special recognition for their help with this memoir are those who wrote sections reflecting the development of ACA priorities, all of which involved the development of academic resources that require computer technologies: Tony Krug, Martin Ramsay, and Rob Hoyt. Their work was heavily dependent on various technologies, and I have continued to remain relatively ignorant about library technologies and computer communications. Ed Welch, who recently retired as president of the University of Charleston (WV), updated me on the status of the Independent College Enterprise (ICE) program he initiated with some initial funding from the ACA.

Lyle Roelofs, president of Berea College, suggested I should write the history of the ACA after I spent about three hours telling him the story of how it developed. Then Pat McPherson, who was vice president at Mellon when I was receiving multi-million-dollar grants from there, read an early version and contacted Mellon to suggest

---

117. Of course, these are just the major ideas she led me through. I would have to write another memoir to recognize all the ideas she had for improving higher education in small private colleges.

Acknowledgements

they ask for a copy. Barbara Robinson is the lawyer who stood up to men who physically towered over her to protect Colonel Ledford's legacy and allow his estate to benefit generations of young people in Appalachia. She read sections about the lawsuit to see that her memory and mine were not too far apart.

Then there is the wonderful Johanna Brownell, who had worked with Dr. Bowen. She recommended so many changes and asked so many questions during her two readings of my memoir that I think it took me as long to make those corrections and add clarifying information as it did to write the narrative the first time. I also owe appreciation to Elizabeth Hayford, who led the Associated Colleges of the Midwest for longer than I led the ACA; after retirement, she co-authored a book with me that was published by Johns Hopkins University Press—*How Boards Lead Small Colleges*. She served on the Advisory Council of the ACA for most of the years it existed, and she twice read this document and shared her views about what makes a successful consortium. Also, Sue Wake, who had worked for over thirty-five years with Jim Taylor, retired president of the University of the Cumberlands, read the memoir to seek out errors no one else had found. Finally, my husband, who had taught English for forty years, agreed, for the first time in our fifty-six years of marriage, to edit the memoir. From his corrections, one could tell he had taught many freshman composition classes.

The last person I trusted to see the manuscript before I sent it off to be published was Rick Kneipper. Rick, when he was with the Jones Day law firm, had been sent to UK by the Exxon Foundation, when the fellowship program was still at UK, to help with questions related to intellectual property rights. Then he served on the ACA Advisory Council from 2000 until 2009. Since his work with the ACA, he has started several companies (including a distillery and Anthelio Healthcare) and currently serves as Chairman of the Board for Aquity Holdings, a technology consulting firm based in Cary, NC. While we have occasionally sent greetings to each other over the years since I retired in 2008, the first time in a long time since we had communicated was in January of 2021, when (of no surprise to those of you who know me) I asked him for a favor--to read the memoir and provide his insights as a friend well acquainted with the ACA under my leadership.

Jane Stephenson, wife of the man who started the Appalachian College Program and then led the founding of the Appalachian College Association based at Warren Wilson, gave me good advice about publishing the memoir myself instead of being at the will of a large publishing house where their ideas can lead your ideas in directions you might never have considered. I was fortunate to find a group of people at Wisdom House who provided invaluable help in getting this book ready to send to the printers. I especially appreciate Ted's patience in letting me make a thousand changes as he worked through the manuscript with me.

This brief acknowledgement can do little to reflect my appreciation for the support during my years at the ACP and ACA and for the help I received in documenting the first two and a half decades the programs enriched the lives of so many faculty and students. None of these people had any reason to want to read a memoir on the ACA as I knew it, but they took the time not only to talk with me about it and read it but also to make recommendations for clarifying what I remember. I hope my memory as it is expressed here honors the twenty-five years of work I devoted to higher education in Appalachia and those who made it possible for the ACA to accomplish so much in so little time. It was certainly an honor to work with those at the member colleges who well deserved every benefit they received and more.

Appendix A

Grants Written and Directed at ACA 1993-2008

Andrew W. Mellon Foundation:
  Faculty Development (21 grants) totaling $21,332,000
  Central Library (12 grants) totaling $9,089,500
  General Administrative Services (five grants) totaling $1,980,000
  Total $32,401,500

(Note: The Mellon database indicates the ACA was awarded 45 grants totaling $33,107,500 between June 1991 and September of 2008, about $706,000 more than I have listed here, but their figure might have included the money awarded to the Appalachian Center between 1980 and 1986 for the Appalachian College Program and funds awarded by Mellon when the ACA was initiated at Warren Wilson.)

Berger Foundation
  International Study (two grants) totaling $3,750,000

Lee B. Ledford Foundation
  Research Grants for Students, $3,719,240 (endowment)

Anonymous Foundation
  Faculty Development, (four grants) totaling $2,650,000

National Science Foundation
  Scholarships and Maintenance of Equipment (four grants) totaling $2,235,386

Department of Commerce
   Technology Training, $649,766

Teagle Foundation
   Assessment and Faculty Development (three grants) totaling $624,650

National Endowment for the Humanities
   Endowment for Fellowships for Faculty, $600,000

Jessie Ball duPont Fund
   Economic Development (with UNC-Chapel Hill), $192,684
   Training for Students in Technology (with VA Tech), $256,235
   Training for Development Officers, $75,000

Culpeper Foundation
   Writing Across the Curriculum, $453,000

Spencer Foundation
   Research on ACA Alumni, $404,000

Surdna Foundation
   Service Learning (two grants) totaling $266,000

Hearst Foundation
   Fellowships for Faculty, $200,000 (three grants for endowment)

Christian A. Johnson Endeavor Fund
   International Programs and Meetings (two grants) totaling $160,000

BB&T Charitable Foundation
   Support for Faculty and Students (two grants) $150,000

Burroughs Wellcome Fund
   Fellowships for Science Faculty, $120,000

Appendix A: Grants Written and Directed at ACA 1993-2008

New York Community Trust
   Grants for Students in Health Sciences (two grants) totaling $105,000

Kenan Foundation
   Endowment for Faculty Fellowships, $100,000

Council on Library and Resources Services
   Restructuring Libraries, $100,000

Others (Wish-You-Well Foundation, Forward Fund, Scripps Howard, Appalachian Regional Commission, Hanes, Travelers Insurance), eight grants totaling $110,500

TOTAL: $49,322,961

Funding awarded to the UK Appalachian College Program (1990 to 1993) included two grants for $280,000 each and one for $150,000 and $25,000 ($735,000) for planning from Mellon; 2 grants for $845,000 and $1,200,000 ($2,045,000) from Pew; $92,000 and $10,000 from Exxon ($102,000); $500,000 from Bingham Foundation; $257,000 from FIPSE for assessment; $10,000 from KY Dept. of Education for UK Theatre Dept. to conduct workshops on producing dramatic productions with limited budgets; $24,000 from TVA for workshops on computer networking; $90,000 from ARC for development of networks; $24,915 from NSF for conference to identify needs of science programs; $107,817 from NSF for training related to networking; and $113,000 for internet connections and $73,495 for Calculus Reform ($319,227); $55,000 plus $357,136 from AT&T for computer labs ($412,136); for a **total of $4,494,363.**

Appendix B

Grants Received and Awards Made from 1993-2008

(These grants were received after the ACA moved its headquarters to Berea, KY, as they were included in the annual reports for those years. The annual reports were received after the memoir narrative was completed.)

1993

The ACA office in Berea was opened. Mellon included science faculty with opportunities for humanities faculty in a $2.8 million grant for fellowships, travel grants, and research with students.

Burroughs Wellcome supported five faculty from five colleges; Mellon fellowships were awarded to 13 faculty from 13 colleges, and 12 faculty-student grants were awarded to those at 11 colleges. Mellon ($50,000) provided funding for a seminar series to encourage collaboration across and within departments of humanities and sciences; Burroughs-Wellcome ($120,000) provided fellowships for science faculty; Anonymous ($450,000) provided fellowships and grants for faculty in education and the fine arts.

1994

Annual reports were issued for 1993-1994 and for 1994-1995, so it was difficult to determine which fellowships were awarded in 1993 for 1994 and which were awarded in 1994 for 1995. However, the number of awards made between 1993 and 1994 and used in

1994 and 1995 did not exceed the number listed here in 1993 and in 1995. The ACA office should have a booklet that was prepared during my tenure listing all fellowships by year.

John Stephenson died in December, and the fellowships in humanities and sciences were named to honor him. The first Stephenson Fellowships were awarded in 1995. Fellowships in education and other professional fields were named to honor Wilma Dykeman and those in fine and performing arts honor Jeanne Ritchie.

1995

Three faculty from three colleges received Burroughs-Wellcome grants; 18 from 15 colleges received Stephenson grants; six from six colleges were funded by McCune; 25 faculty from 14 colleges received student-faculty awards. Twenty-seven colleges participated in workshops and meetings with consultants related to planned giving. The repair service provided by NSF funding to UK continued; the ARC funded 50+ students from 22 colleges to participate in the Washington Center's seminars. NSF funded a consultant to research the use of technology in teaching at 26 ACA colleges; the report provided basic information for other funding related to the use of technology in teaching.

1996

A $1.5 million grant from Mellon brought major attention to teaching with technology. Grants from Mellon, McCune, and Burroughs-Wellcome enabled 32 fellowships to be awarded to faculty at 23 colleges (totaling $636,500) and 31 student-faculty grants were awarded to those at 16 colleges ($177,357). The repair van continued to operate; 30+ students from 17 colleges attended the Washington Center's program with ARC funding; 25 ACA colleges participated in the ACA's contract with Auburn University to develop a profile with both longitudinal and comparative information. In addition to the $1.5 million from Mellon, Scripps-Howard gave $5,000 to place volunteers in the ACA office; Elderhostel provided $60,656 for program oversight; a US Depart of Commerce grant of $649,726 gave ACA colleges in eight communities resources to make information technology accessible in their areas. An example of the creative thinking of the colleges was the WV Wesleyan solution to finding a place with public access 24/7—a local motel.

1997

The major focus in 1997 was the strategic plan approved by the ACA Executive Committee to fulfill a requirement for an application to NEH to establish an endowment. Reflecting on the fact that the ACA assets were continuing to grow, presidents, deans, and faculty were surveyed to determine what was most valued and what was still most needed. Fellowships and chances to work with others across the ACA were highly valued. Presidents liked that involvement in most projects was voluntary. All member colleges had received more financial benefits than they had paid in dues, and most projects had allowed the colleges to move more quickly into new areas of education. Foundation representatives had praise for the leadership and management of the ACA.

Focus groups indicated there was no competition among members for students and none with the ACA for funding. (However, as one president said privately to me: "Our colleges don't compete with each other for students until those students decide to go to a private college in our region." Also, by 2008, when I retired, one concern of the presidents—especially those at the colleges most financially insecure—was that the ACA was attracting financial support they might have received if the ACA had not been in the picture.)

In addition to continuing current benefits, such as fellowships, an emphasis on international experiences and service learning and more chances for collaboration were priorities. A consultant, Bethany Baxter, recommended that the ACA present annual reports reflecting the financial benefits derived by each member college and establish an advisory council to provide ideas for projects or programs that would benefit most members. Every year following this Strategic Plan, at the meeting of presidents and academic deans, the ACA office distributed a report indicating the benefits provided by the ACA for each member college and the dues paid by each college. The first of these studies indicated that for every dollar the schools paid in dues, they received at least $7 in benefits. The first Advisory Council members included Edgar Beckham, formerly with Ford Foundation; Tish Emerson, Mellon; Elizabeth Hayford, president of the ACM; Dick Johnson, formerly with Exxon; Bob Watson, Head of Undergraduate Research at NSF; John C. Williams, Regional BB&T President for the Tri-States; and Rudy Abramson, co-editor of the *Encyclopedia of Appalachia*, and formerly Washington, D.C. reporter for the *Los Angeles Times*. (If "formerly" is not included with a name, the person was with the organization listed at the time he or she served on the Council.)

The ACA awarded a lot of faculty and student-faculty grants: Stephenson Fellowships (32 from 27 colleges = almost $500,000); Jean Ritchie and Wilma Dykeman Fellowships (15 from 12 colleges = over $250,000); student-faculty grants (32 from 19 colleges = $163,100). The total (about $900,000) would no longer be possible once the funding had to be drawn from endowment income. New grants included $1.8 million from Mellon to provide all ACA colleges with access to JSTOR; $2.7 million from Mellon to continue fellowships and grants for Stephenson Fellowships for faculty in arts and sciences; $600,000 from McCune for fellowships and grants in arts and education; $453,000 from Culpeper for Writing-Across-the-Curriculum projects; $3,500 from the Travelers Foundation for general administration; and $59,717 from Elderhostel for administration of the ACA office, which, at that time, included KY Elderhostel. The University of KY received $400,481 from NSF to continue the repair van providing repair services for ACA colleges.

1998

The annual report includes a list of accomplishments by faculty at ACA colleges who had received grants from the ACA or participated in ACA events: four completed doctoral degrees; 12 completed residency requirements and/or courses leading to the doctoral degree; 31 faculty who had terminal degrees conducted research to update and upgrade their teaching materials; 28 faculty and 52 students collaborated on research projects; 147 faculty made presentations at professional meetings (travel grants); 15 faculty collaborated on the development of a course on entrepreneurship; 283 faculty gained skills in teaching with technology at workshops; 59 faculty collaborated with faculty from other institutions to develop teaching materials that used new technologies; 38 faculty participated in an ACA workshop on community service and social justice; 93 librarians participated in ACA workshops; 170 faculty learned new techniques for teaching writing in the ACA Writing-Across-the-Curriculum program; eight colleges brought new electronic infrastructure to their local communities with the grant from the US Dept. of Commerce; almost 400 faculty from 31 colleges attended the first ACA Technology Summit, the culminating event for the over one-million-dollar grant to help faculty learn the technology important to instruction in all fields—a Summit which impressed Mellon so much they awarded $3.9 million for future work with technology and teaching. Mellon funding enabled the ACA to give JSTOR to member colleges.

VA Tech received a grant from Jessie Ball duPont for $43,600 to train students from ACA colleges in workshops at Tech to serve their colleges as Student Technical Assistants. (Grants to VA Tech and UNC from duPont were awarded for those universities to work with the ACA since the ACA is not a duPont-approved institution.) Working with faculty and staff at these and other major research universities has proved beneficial in ways not anticipated prior to those experiences, such as nurturing of ACA students for graduate study, providing surplus equipment to ACA colleges, having university faculty serve as outside evaluators and guest speakers for various programs at ACA colleges, etc. The NEH Challenge Grant was awarded at $600,000 and required a match of $1.8 million; within a year $10 million had been raised.

1999

A Steering Committee for the ACA librarians' organization which fosters collaboration in various areas of library services was established. Mellon funding enabled the development of a toolbox to be used in teaching research methods. Each library received ScholarStat software, which facilitates comparison of data across libraries—information important to accreditation. Awards (from $290 to $2,447) were given to encourage events to help faculty understand the new technologies, and a database of faculty involved in various aspects of teaching with technology was started. JSTOR was available at 29 ACA colleges, and multiple other collections were made available at reduced costs.

The Writing-Across-the-Curriculum project was featured as a strand at the Technology Summit. Writing Centers had been developed at 14 colleges. One group presented at a National WAC Event (where Harvard faculty also presented). New Student Technology Assistants (114) were trained, along with 13 Intern Trainers and 24 STA Supervisors. Twenty-two ACA colleges then had STAs. Progress was made on the Center for Appalachian Entrepreneurship Studies—a virtual concept intended to serve as a base for resources related to the teaching of entrepreneurship. Sixteen faculty from 15 colleges received fellowships: nine for $30,000—seven for work toward the Ph.D., including residency. Twelve faculty-student grants were awarded to faculty at ten ACA colleges. Over $194,000 was awarded for travel grants.

The first members of the ACA Advisory Council attended the annual meeting of academic deans and presidents. Five major foundations and roughly 200 individuals contributed to the endowment. Jane Stephenson (wife of John) gave $10,000; one faculty member at a small ACA college gave $1,000, which was 10% of royalties received from the sale of the book completed during his fellowship. Mellon gave $4 million; about 200 individuals gave a total of about $22,000. Almost 60% of fellowship recipients contributed, some more than once. Hearst gave $200,000. Kenan gave $100,000. Our Anonymous Foundation gave $1.5 million.

2000

Fifteen Stephenson Fellowships were awarded to faculty at 11 colleges, and four Dykeman Fellowships went to faculty at three ACA colleges. The total awarded was $358,001 (including $10,000 from a Culpeper Grant); $193,222 was awarded for travel grants. A $30,000 fellowship was awarded to an ACA faculty member for research in chemistry funded by NSF through a grant to University of TN. (This example represents a benefit of having the graduate deans involved. The UT grant provided funding for two ACA faculty each year of the grant.) Thirteen Ledford Scholarships enabled 32 students and

14 faculty from 11 colleges to conduct student-faculty research. The STA program at VA Tech had ended, but 52 students from 16 colleges with 16 supervisors at those colleges and seven trainers attended a similar training effort at Lincoln Memorial University. Future workshops were expected to be held at other ACA colleges across the region.

Collaboration with the University of Maryland's Appalachian Laboratory provided opportunities for ACA faculty and students to learn new skills related to environmental research. Faculty from the University of the South, Ferrum, and WV Wesleyan established local watershed research sites with funding provided (including that for equipment), and a workshop was held on ecosystem ecology for 20 ACA faculty. ACA students received internships for summer research at the Appalachian Lab and the three ACA research sites focusing on watersheds. Funds were available to give ACA collaborators the chance to bring small classes to the Appalachian Lab; faculty from the Lab visited ACA colleges to present seminars on their research.

Technology training continued: 574 people from 32 colleges attended 18 grant-sponsored workshops. Forty-three information tech directors and faculty attended an international Conference on College Teaching and Learning in Florida; 278 faculty, students and administrators attended the ACA Technology Summit. Pre-conference workshops on teaching entrepreneurship and writing proposals for NSF attracted some who didn't attend the Summit.

The major focus this year was on the Mellon grant to encourage faculty collaboration across ACA campuses: eight projects encompassed 18 colleges. Topics ranged from revising individual courses to preparing and teaching interdisciplinary courses and using electronic technology to enhance laboratory instruction. Disciplinary groups were established with faculty serving as coordinators.

The Central Library continued to expand services: 65 grants were provided to librarians to attend technology workshops. Three workshops for librarians attracted 114 from 32 colleges. The Digital Library of Appalachia was funded at $50,000 for six libraries to learn digitizing archival collections at ACA colleges. Twenty-eight contracts for collective purchasing saved ACA libraries more than $2 million in database fees. NEH gave $20,000 for grants for preservation programs for archival collections in ACA libraries.

The Writing-Across-the-Disciplines program held workshops (attended by 60 faculty) and a workshop and an online peer-tutoring manual was completed to train writing center tutors.

The Alumni Study funded by Spencer and Mellon began; 23 ACA colleges and six state universities participated. Drs. Ernie Pascarella and Pat Terenzini developed the survey and ACT administered it. Pascarella and Terenzini oversaw the analysis of data collected. Alumni from classes of 1975, 1985, and 1995 were surveyed. Two workshops funded by Mellon helped women wanting to advance their careers in college administration; three women attended the HERS Summer Institute at Bryn Mawr College.

2001

Sixteen fellows from 11 colleges were funded ($288,200) and 85 faculty from 28 colleges had travel grants to make presentations in 25 states and six foreign countries. Eleven colleges collaborated on an art exhibit and workshops in art (funded from the Canon Fund). Four faculty from four colleges completed doctoral degrees at UNC, Vanderbilt, VA Tech, Ohio U; two from two other colleges became ABD at UT and Columbia.

Two grants awarded by the Berger Foundation (totaling $3,750,000) enabled faculty and students to study abroad. Four short-terms seminars were conducted in Europe and Asia, and 45 students and 20 faculty from 17 ACA colleges participated in those seminars. Four students received grants of $8,000 to spend a semester in London.

NSF funding of $270,000 provided scholarships of $3,125 for 20 students from 12 colleges; the graduate deans from the research universities affiliated with the ACA met with those students and made presentations about job and graduate school opportunities.

Two workshops were held in Pittsburgh, hosted by the Pittsburgh Opera. They were designed to help faculty learn how to incorporate the arts into academic disciplines other than art, music and theatre and how to bring the arts to the public schools. Participants were given tours of backstage and attended an opera as well as a play held at another Pittsburgh site. Leaders came from arts organizations in Pittsburgh as well as from colleges and universities outside ACA. Being in Pittsburgh during the Christmas season was a special experience in itself.

Funding from Spencer enabled 13 faculty from nine colleges to be ACA Research Fellows and complete research projects using data from the Alumni Study—which surveyed 12,400 graduates from 23 ACA colleges.

New collaborative projects included a program to study retention and student success; a program for orientation of new faculty (modeled after the one at Berea where new faculty and staff travel to eastern KY to visit churches, schools, and other elements of the culture from which many students at ACA colleges come); a conference to prepare member colleges to develop international studies programs that can be shared; a plan to hire one strategic planning expert to work across the campuses but to develop local plans; a workshop on financial aid; a central human resources office for West Virginia colleges; and a project where five colleges centralized administrative computing—the Institutional Collaborative Endeavor (ICE). A workshop at the University of PA's Wharton School of Business, led by Bob Zemsky, encouraged four ACA colleges to consider new areas for collaboration: a collaborative website; a strategy for involving young alumni of participating ACA colleges; collaboration in distributive learning; and consolidated services in career services.

The grant for increasing the use of technology in teaching was extended for three more years. Six new collaborative courses were developed bringing the total of small grants to 17 involving 77 faculty from 26 ACA colleges. The Summit continued with 257 participants from 32 of the 33 colleges. Writing across the Curriculum was merged into the effort to encourage collaboration and 20 colleges continued to be involved. The Student Technical Assistants (STA) program continued.

The focus on libraries continued to expand: six colleges completed the Instructional Toolbox; nine colleges received funding to update faculty on library technology; the Digital Library of Appalachia received $50,000 for a pilot project involving six ACA colleges; three workshops (on public services, technical services, and library administration) attracted librarians from all ACA colleges, and some attended all three. Forty-five purchasing contracts saved every ACA college from $19,000 to $167,000. The librarians wrote a proposal to fully develop the ACA Central Library requesting $5.3 million; and the first $1,050,000 was received with additional funding to follow. Mellon decided the Central Library project had grown past the point that a half-time director was sufficient. When Tony Krug was asked if he would work full-time for the ACA, he said he needed a more secure job than one on "soft" money because he had a family to support. When Bowen learned this, he said, "We'll endow the position." And they did.

2002

Seventeen faculty from 13 colleges received fellowships ($293,967); 80 faculty from 28 colleges had travel grants to make presentations in 25 states and 12 foreign countries. Sixteen faculty were funded for research projects that crossed institutions. Funding from NSF provided scholarships of $3,125 for 40 Students. Mellon established an endowment for the Central Library at $2.9 million to endow Tony's salary and continue collections such as JSTOR. Leadership Education Advancing Development (LEAD) provided scholarships to HERS Summer Institute at Bryn Mawr, and the participants then held workshops in their local regions. Thirty-eight Distinguished Scholars from 16 colleges received scholarships of $3,125 from the NSF grant.

Five students received $8,000 for a semester in London. This semester in London program has encouraged a group of ACA colleges to form the Private College Consortium for International Studies. Five seminars were scheduled to be held in Europe, South Africa, and Asia and 66 students and 23 faculty from 14 ACA colleges were scheduled to participate. Five students were funded to participate in the Washington Center's internship program.

Thirteen Research Fellows from eight colleges received funding with three workshops on uses for the data collected during the study of ACA alumni; 11 faculty were funded to make presentations of their research at the Association for Institutional Research and the Appalachian Studies Association.

Writing Across the Curriculum hosted a summer institute for 34 writing program directors and faculty from 15 disciplines representing 14 colleges.

A faculty member from Emory & Henry who had received numerous grants served half-time to help ACA faculty and students develop proposals and a database of faculty-student research at ACA colleges. An ACA Public Relations Council was organized and led by the president of Lincoln Memorial (Nancy Moody) to sponsor three meetings and a professional development workshop that drew 25 people from 12 colleges; one focus was coordinating news releases.

The Technology Summit attracted 336 from 33 colleges; STA training attracted 50 students and 21 supervisors. The ACA Virtual Center enabled the various discipline groups to work together without leaving their home campuses.

The student-faculty Art Exhibit of 29 works from 11 colleges was held at ten locations in four states, providing public recognition of the art being created at ACA colleges and opportunities for students to learn more about art techniques. Again, the Canon funds covered associated costs related to preparing the exhibits.

The third Arts Integration Seminar was held at the Pittsburgh Opera and funded by the McCune Foundation. Twenty-six faculty from 14 ACA colleges attended to learn how to incorporate the arts into college classes and how to develop methods for teaching art to elementary and secondary school students. The first ACA Opera Tour brought members of the Pittsburgh Opera (two singers, a musical director, a stage director, and an education expert) to four ACA campuses (Ferrum, Sewanee, Bethany and Carson-Newman) for two-day residencies that included seminars, rehearsals, opera improvisation and a full performance of *Il Segreto di Suysanna*.

The Central Library received $1.9 million from Mellon. The Digital Library of Appalachia was completed with all colleges participating. (Membership varied and was as high as 37 with 33 being the lowest.) NEH funding of $22,797 went to five ACA libraries for their digital collections. All libraries now have access to a minimum of 30,000 electronic book titles. Workshops on JSTOR attracted 34 from 23 colleges; the annual meeting of librarians in public service attracted 42 from 34 ACA colleges; the annual meeting for library administrators brought together 35 directors and deans from 34 colleges. A dues structure and the library endowment cover annual Archive Capital Fees and portions of the Annual Access Fee for the JSTOR Arts and Sciences collections that include over 100 journal titles in the liberal arts. Individual libraries can add specialized collections, such as General Science and Ecology & Botany.

2003

The Fellowship Endowment had grown to over $8 million. Fellowships were awarded to 16 faculty from ten colleges; travel grants went to 52 faculty from 23 ACA colleges to make presentations at professional meetings. From funding for the Central Library two librarians from two colleges received Alice Emerson fellowships to work toward terminal degrees. One faculty member participated in the NSF research program in chemistry at UT—funded by the UT grant. Student-faculty awards went to 40 students and faculty from 15 colleges.

After roughly four years, the lawsuit involving the estate of Lee B. Ledford in New York was settled (by Barbara Robinson—a pro bono lawyer Bowen recruited), and the ACA received $3.7 million for an endowment to support student-faculty research. West Point was the other beneficiary of the settlement. An appreciation dinner was held to honor Barbara, and funding remaining from the Canon endowment was used to give Robinson awards to two students at ACA colleges who had been accepted at a law school for the next year. In later years, Barbara herself provided funding for the awards, and after several years, students who had attended law school with funding from a Robinson award were invited by Barbara to spend several days in New York observing lawyers working in a major city. Ten Ledford Scholars from seven colleges were named to conduct research with guidance from a mentor from his/her home institution; each received between $1,300 and $4,100. The Student Technical Assistants' training continued with about 40 students participating.

NSF funded 27 STEM scholarships for students at ten ACA colleges majoring in math or computer science or engineering; each scholarship provided $3,125 to help cover tuition, fees, books, supplies, and equipment for the students.

To emphasize the importance of various legal and safety precautions, an International Summit was held with representatives from 18 ACA colleges. Presentations covered liability issues, crisis management, health and safety, programmatic issues, institutional cross-cultural initiatives and requirements, service learning, and how to set up a short-term study abroad program. An online Resource Center was developed to strengthen international study on ACA campuses. Two hundred twenty faculty, staff, and students from 30 ACA college traveled to Mexico at different points of the year, and a two-week trip included 19 professors from 14 colleges going to Mexico to study "Art, Architecture, and Culture." A trip to the United Kingdom and the Netherlands to study education for handicapped students was led by Bluefield College with participants from four other colleges; a trip to Vietnam was led by

Wheeling with participants from two other colleges; a trip to the United Kingdom to study art and art history was led by VA Intermont with participants from three other colleges; a trip to Malawi, led by Union College, allowed participants from a total of four colleges to work on a watershed project with faculty and students from the U. of Malawi. Only Warren Wilson and Emory & Henry participated in two of the travel groups. In a two-week study experience in Spain, 14 faculty focused on religions and other elements of the culture to develop courses about the country.

A new Mellon grant provided fellowships for 18 faculty from 17 colleges to participate in Salzburg Seminars on topics such as Leadership Across Boundaries/Borders, Migration, Race and Ethnicity in Europe. Seminars held in Europe and South America attracted 55 students and 27 faculty from 20 ACA colleges. Mellon funding allowed the ACA to create "Shadow Grants," which enabled 16 faculty to travel to four continents to shadow an experienced study abroad director in preparing for and leading a successful tour. These experiences should help the ACA create study abroad experiences in which any student at an ACA college could participate. The ACA explored possibilities for ACA students to travel with groups outside the ACA who were taking international study trips, such as the Associated Colleges of the Midwest, but the costs were prohibitive.

The second tour of the Pittsburgh Opera performers was held with residencies at five colleges (Alice Lloyd, Davis & Elkins, Mars Hill, U. of Charleston, and Lee) and nearby colleges co-hosting. This tour brought a performance of *La Grande Tanta* as well as a variety of workshops, seminars, and classes. Total attendance at all the events was 2,428.

The first week-long Teaching & Learning Institute was held. Forty-seven faculty from 21 colleges brought syllabi to revise working with experts in the use of technology, embedded assessment, collaborative learning, etc. Each Institute will be held on an ACA college campus. The Writing-across-the-Curriculum Program started in 1997 continued with workshops hosted by the Knight Institute for Writing, and by faculty from Georgetown and Cornell. Twenty ACA colleges participated.

The Central Library continued to provide professional development for librarians and training for faculty and staff to assure they can use the new resources available. The Digital Library of Appalachia was made available via the Internet. Tony Krug, head ACA librarian, provided a chart showing that ACA colleges now had access to library books, videos, periodicals and references like those at major research universities.

The 2003 initiatives in the Teaching and Technology Program included workshops to train technology leaders in certain disciplines; the STA training continued; and WebCT course management software was researched. The annual Summit had more than 300 participants. The U. of Charleston (WV) led Institutional Cooperative Endeavor (ICE) continued to enable the sharing of technology for back-office operations to reduce costs for individual colleges. A guest artist, Michael Chitwood, toured eight campuses for readings and seminars with students. Eight courses were collaboratively developed; workshops were held on topics such as Metromedia Flash and low-cost, low band-width methods for enhancing courses through the internet. Berea College maintained a shared DS3 line to manage the 39 servers and software necessary for the ACA Central Library. The ACA purchased a WebCT Vista site license and developed a laptop lab for loan to ACA colleges. The Tech Team planned to support ACA students enrolled in internet-based courses offered by VA Tech with on-campus mentors at the home ACA colleges, but the ACA Executive Committee cancelled those plans.

Thirteen Research Fellows continued to complete research projects with the data collected from the alumni study. Ten studies were presented at national conferences. Two LEAD conferences addressed issues facing women administrators. Over the three years LEAD workshops were held and a total of 170 women participated.

To summarize: at this point, we had more than 20 on-going grant-funded programs with a budget of $4.5 million and an endowment of over $14 million; $8 million was available in new grant funds and more than $4 million was requested in pending proposals. My goal was to have five grant proposals being prepared at any time with at least three under review. In 2003, over 500 faculty, librarians, and administrators participated in more than 100 ACA workshops involving new pedagogies and enhanced curricula. From an original staff of three in 1993, in 2003, we had 12 full-time and three part-time employees, most funded by grants related to specific projects.

Eighteen fellowships were awarded to faculty from 13 colleges; and 58 from 27 colleges received travel grants to make presentations at professional seminars. Also, two librarians from two colleges received year-long fellowships for graduate study; and two faculty from two ACA colleges received grants from UT to participate in their NSF Research Grant. Seventy students-faculty research grants were awarded ($243,082); 55 students and 27 faculty from 20 colleges had international study experiences; and ten students from six ACA colleges had Ledford grants for research with faculty.

David Baldacci was the keynote speaker at the annual meeting of presidents and deans; not only did he not charge for his presentation, but he also gave the ACA $5,000 to fund the Appalachian

Artists Series.

NSF funding provided 54 Noyce scholarships of $7,500 to encourage students majoring in STEM subjects to become teachers in public schools in central Appalachia. In a separate grant, NSF funded 30 two-year scholarships of $2,750 each year to encourage students to major in STEM fields as CSTEM Scholars.

Sixty-five faculty from 28 colleges participated in the week-long Teaching & Learning Institute. The Ledford Scholars program provided up to $4,000 per award to support undergraduate research mentored by faculty; 40 students were trained to be STA's. Over 300 faculty and students who had received awards from ACA attended the Technology Summit.

The Central Library collection reached 55,000 e-books and seven major reference databases. Each campus had received a benefit of more than $1 million in core collections and services. Some librarians had more online volumes than they had on their shelves.

Christian A. Johnson added $160,000 to the $3,750,000 provided by the Berger Foundation to extend opportunities for study abroad.

2004

In 2004, member colleges received over $4 million in benefits. Opportunities for faculty included 21 fellowships and 69 travel grants; the total awarded was $376,511; $243,082 provided funding for 70 students scholars. International study trips for 55 students and 27 faculty from 20 member institutions were funded by Berger. Eighteen fellowships were awarded to faculty from 13 different ACA colleges; two librarians (from two additional colleges) were awarded Emerson Fellowships for graduate study, and two faculty (from two other colleges) were awarded grants by UT to participate in an NSF grant there. In all, 22 faculty from 17 colleges received fellowships. Ten students from six colleges received Ledford grants to do research at their home campuses under mentorship by local faculty. Noyce and CSEM Scholars (with NSF funding) were encouraged to major in science disciplines or to certify to teach in science fields. We learned that one difficulty in awarding Noyce Scholarships (even though each award is $7,500/year) is that students receiving those awards must be tracked after graduation to be sure they fulfill the commitment to teach in a high-need geographic region for at least two years for each scholarship received. We were able to do that with all but two scholars, and NSF seemed pleased we were able to track that many. A total of 60 students benefitted from the multiple opportunities provided by the ACA.

Pamela Duncan visited seven ACA campuses as part of the Appalachian Artists Series; Thomas Rain Crowe spoke at eight campuses. Almost 300 attended the annual Summit as the number of presentations increased from about 70 to 100. Faculty and deans had started comparing it to the annual homecoming where "everyone gathers to reconnect and inspire each other." Sixty-five faculty attended the summer Teaching & Learning Institute.

Mellon awarded the Central Library $1.2 million to enable all the colleges to have Artstor. A series of workshops and internships provides continuing professional development for the more than 200 librarians at ACA colleges. Over 80 databases were selected and configured to meet the needs of individual colleges; the Central Library also provided a collection by discipline of several thousand annotated links to websites and a digital reference system. The Central Library staff worked with VA Tech to develop a program for Instructional Technology Assistants (ITAs similar to but not the same as Student Technical Assistants--STAs). Seventy-two students received training to be Instructional Technology Assistants. Students learned to help faculty develop instructional units. Packet shapers were provided to colleges requesting them so that high priority Internet traffic could receive a larger portion of bandwidth available.

The first annual ACA Conference on e-Learning was held. Topics included course sharing across institutions and using technology to improve communications with students. Over 1,700 students received online training for Microsoft and Macromedia certification, and almost 70 ACA faculty completed an online course taught by VA Tech on internet theory and use. (These training courses did not carry academic credit.) A single license for course development and learning management software was shared by 11 member colleges. About 40 students were prepared to work as Student Technical Assistants.

Funding from the Surdna Foundation ($266,000) provided scholarships for students to develop leadership skills through service projects in their local communities; the goal was to develop a reservoir of new graduates who had demonstrated commitment to and experience in Appalachia. For most ACA colleges, the Surdna Citizen Scholars program was a natural addition to what the institutions were already doing to encourage commitments to service.

2005

A total of $395,443 was awarded to 22 faculty for fellowships and travel grants and student-faculty research projects. And over $1 million was awarded to students for scholarships and research grants. Almost 100 students received awards. Forty-two students from 12 colleges received Ledford grants (for research with faculty on their campuses); 22 students from 16 colleges received funding from the Surdna Foundation to work within teams of students, faculty and community agency leaders; 12 students from ten colleges received Noyce Scholarships of

$7,500; and 20 students from ten colleges received CSEM Scholarships of $3,125. Students and faculty benefited from Berger Scholarships: one group went to China to study the country that was becoming a major economic player in the world; another went to Eastern Europe to study nationalism in the former Hapsburg Empire; another went to South America for an interdisciplinary study of climate, geology, ecology, history, sociology, and politico-economic issues; another went to India to study the diversity and how 52 ethnic groups have preserved their traditions. Faculty groups studied Global Citizenship at a Salzburg Seminar; another faculty group went to China to study the religious, political, economic, and international realities there.

The annual week-long Teaching & Learning Institute featured Peggy Maki, one of the nation's leading assessment experts; the emphasis was on engaging students. The Technology Summit attracted over 400 participants. The technology of the ACA moved from a server-centric model to a learner-centric model. With Mellon funding, the ACA explored WebCT Vista for course content at small colleges to post assignments and supplemental reading materials and provide and outlines and discussions between faculty and students. At the peak of the ACA test of WebCT, 14 schools and 20% of ACA 's faculty participated. But it became clear that WebCT could not be sustained by most of the member colleges. Some wanted to continue using it, but many could not afford it even though they liked the system. The solution was Learning Activities Management Program (LAMP). Open-source software has no licensing fees; the software can be modified as needed. With students trained as Instructional Technology Assistants, faculty learned to use the new technology, and online instruction continued the training. Element K provided online training with academic databases, allowing teachers to make assignments and monitor the progress of their students. The ACA negotiated $15 for ACA members (compared to the full price of $828/license). A Technology Council was formed to follow the development of trends in instructional technology. The Annual Meeting on Library Administration featured Deanna Marcum, chief operating officer at the Library of Congress and an expert on building digital libraries. A new grant from Mellon brought the library endowment to $5.2 million.

A workshop at Emory & Henry on Advanced Teaching of Math and Science (ATOMS) was supported by Branch Banking and Trust, the ACA, and NSF. Associated was a summer camp for rising ninth, tenth and eleventh graders developed by a Noyce Scholar.

The total ACA endowment reached $15 million; the Summit attracted 400 participants. Data reported in the annual report for 2005 indicated that, since the move to Berea, benefits distributed annually to faculty and students had increased five times—to roughly $5 million, not counting benefits for libraries. Operating costs had remained at roughly $1 million (including expenses related to fundraising). Salaries for project directors were generally covered by the grants awarded for each project. Amounts received by each college reflected the impact of having a staff person assigned responsibility for submitting requests to the ACA; Ferrum College, the only one with such a staff person, had received approximately $300,000 more than any other member college. The chart at the end of this book indicates that by 2008, Ferrum had received over $2 million.

2006

The endowment had grown to $21 million, and over $1.4 million was awarded to 73 faculty and 131 students. Librarians and technology staff were involved in multiple ACA events, such as the Summit and training for Student Technical Assistants and Instructional Technology Assistants. Fellowships were awarded to 24 faculty at

19 colleges; Ledford Scholarships were presented to 33 students from 16 colleges to conduct research with their faculty mentors; Noyce Scholarships were awarded to 21 students at 13 colleges; 47 CSEM Scholars were named at 18 colleges; a Robinson Scholar would enter law school and receive a second-year fellowship if progress was made satisfactory. Surdna Citizen Scholars (27 from 11 colleges) completed service-learning projects.

Summit participation exceeded 500, with every ACA college represented. The technology staff developed a partnership with IBM to provide software and training for ACA faculty; IBM had grown concerned about the pool of potential employees for the company. Twenty-one faculty from eight ACA colleges participated. Since 2000, the Student Technology Assistants program had trained 386 students from 28 colleges. The program for this year was revised to include an Advanced Student Technology Assistants program to help students and staff at member colleges learn more about network security, lab software deployment, and network configuration. The LAMP colleges decided on Saki as their course management system, a free open-source learning management tool. A company named Element K provided online training in technical topics, such as Microsoft Word, Excel, PowerPoint, Adobe Photoshop, Illustrator, Dreamweaver; the total available was over 1,500 courses. ACA was able to consolidate its buying power; 3,712 licenses had been purchased by 2006 with a value of over $3 million.

The Teaching & Learning Conference focused on how to identify student learning styles, develop appropriate teaching strategies, and determine appropriate assessments for those strategies. The institute enrolled 72 faculty from 28 ACA colleges. Leaders for the week-long event included six nationally recognized experts in retention, teaching strategies and assessment.

Now in its tenth year of service, the Central Library was named the William G. Bowen Central Library of Appalachia to honor Dr. Bowen with recognition for his interest in and dedication to the small colleges of central Appalachia. A group of college presidents from the ACA visited with the ACA president to present Dr. Bowen with a collection of letters acknowledging the value of the work of the ACA projects that Mellon had funded and to announce the official name of the William G. Bowen Central Library of Appalachia. With a core collection in place, the focus of the BCLA was to increase usage of the library resources; each ACA college has a librarian who attends at least one event sponsored by the Central Library each year. This year, about 500 faculty received training and meetings that explained the resources available. Access to the library resources was enhanced by a shared catalog and proxy servers. In 2006, 16 libraries received assistance from the shared catalog; and in 2007, another eight will be added. By 2008, 28 libraries are expected to be participating in the shared catalog.

Three groups of Berger Scholars traveled to a Salzburg Seminar on Global Citizenship. In 2006, faculty and students completed trips to China (two groups), Italy, Germany, and South Africa.

2007

Mellon, to prepare for the planned transition with Alice Brown's retirement next year, endowed a position for a vice president of academic programs to help assure programs continue to evolve and the new president will have time for the fundraising that promises to continue to increase.

The total amount awarded to 24 faculty at 19 colleges for fellowships was $332,800. For research with a faculty mentor from their colleges, 27 students from 16 colleges received funding. NSF Noyce Scholars (nine at eight colleges) and CSEM Scholars (34 from eight colleges) were named; three colleges had both Noyce and CSEM Scholars. One student received a Robinson Scholarship (with funding for a second year if progress was made) to attend law school. Twenty-seven students from nine colleges participated in service-learning projects with funding from Surdna; and Richard Couto (from the University of Richmond) conducted an evaluation of the program. Couto concluded students who had not been involved in community service were more satisfied with their education than those who had; those who had participated realized their college was not really preparing them for the problems that exist in rural regions.

This was the year that funding from the New York Community Trust was awarded. The Oakley Logan and Ethel Witherspoon Alexander Scholars were supported through that trust. These funds were available only to students from Kentucky and West Virginia (homes of the two donors) and were intended to encourage students to major in medical fields. Funding was received by 15 students at seven colleges. The Trust had contacted the Appalachian Regional Commission in D.C., seeking an appropriate non-profit to administer the income (anticipated to be about $100,000 per year) to students majoring in health science or medical fields; ARC recommended the ACA. One goal of the first strategic plan developed by the ACA for a grant submission to NEH was "national recognition." This gift from the New York Community Trust indicates the ACA had gained national recognition.

This was also the year that the Office of Economic and Business Development at UNC-Chapel Hill and the ACA received funding from Jessie Ball duPont to initiate the Appalachian Colleges Community Economic Development Partnership (ACCEDP), a program where four ACA member institutions were selected to build, with the help of faculty from UNC, strong communities by attracting strong businesses to Appalachia. (ACA could not submit proposals to that foundation since the ACA was not on the list of the intended beneficiaries.) Students received stipends to work with their colleges and local communities on a mutually identified project geared to strengthen the relationship between the two and increase the economic power of the region. The four colleges selected were Ferrum, KY Christian, King, and Mars Hill and nine students received stipends; a college in West Virginia submitted a proposal to participate, but the UNC committee (who indicated they had really wanted to work with that community) felt the request to participate was exceptionally weak. What was exceptional about the project was that it was among multiple proposals from UNC that sought funding from duPont, but since that university could submit one proposal that term, the chancellor at UNC selected the ACA proposal. His rationale was that this project would give UNC a presence in four states outside of North Carolina.

2008

The last report during my term indicated it was for 2007-2008. It indicates a problem I faced in deciding what awards were awarded for what year. Most annual reports were for one year, but 2005-2006 and 2007-2008 were each for parts of two years. Also, since I never anticipated writing this summary, I did not make sure that all reports were relatively consistent in the information provided. The annual reports that were published after I retired indicated that the fellowship program remained strong. Although additional funding was not sought for the fellowship endowment, the income generated has kept the number awarded at a consistent level. This endowment has given faculty a lot of control over their academic scholarship, and having the graduate deans involved in the selection process has kept the quality of research funded high. While that scholarship may not be highly important to the college of the fellow, it clearly has been important to faculty. Many, many times I heard from faculty about what a blessing funding from the ACA had been—and they had boasted to their friends teaching at more prestigious colleges about the opportunities from the ACA that were not available to those at many other institutions.

Appendix C

Total Benefits Versus Dues Paid 1990-2008

(This list does not include benefits derived from affiliation with the Bowen Central Library. Also, when I checked the math, I noticed that in each case—except the total—of the return per dollar paid, each amount should be one dollar more than that indicated. Thus $13.89 should be $14.89; $15.99 should be $16.99; etc. I have not changed the figures because I don't know if there is a reason for this discrepancy, and no one seems to know who prepared this chart so I couldn't go to the source to learn a reason for the discrepancies.)

ACA Institution	Total Dues	Total Benefits	$ Return per $ Paid
Alderson-Broaddus	66,833	995,298	13.89
Alice Lloyd	49,384	838,847	15.99
Berea	134,802	1,471,549	9.92
Bethany	76,571	616,809	7.06
Bluefield	68,692	965,749	13.06
Brevard (joined 2003)	35,049	591,299	15.87
Bryan	52,513	649,656	11.37
Campbellsville	123,683	983,100	6.95
Carson-Newman	173,024	1,669,658	8.65
U. of the Cumberlands	128,061	1,010,469	6.89
Davis & Elkins	57,034	994,339	16.43

Emory & Henry	86,181	1,512,235	16.55
Ferrum	95,476	2,183,688	21.87
KY Christian (joined 1996)	42,711	589,388	12.80
King	59,148	1,007,148	16.03
Lee	274,487	1,433,936	4.26
Lees-McRae	70,603	763,095	9.81
Lenoir-Rhyne	29,815	194,500	5.52
Lincoln Memorial	144,859	1,015,176	6.01
Lindsey Wilson	129,592	841,259	5.49
Mars Hill	115,662	1,306,870	10.30
Maryville	87,862	1,147,607	12.06
Milligan	79,904	1,067,765	12.36
Montreat	80,685	866,810	9.74
Ohio Valley	37,939	737,778	18.45
Pikeville	89,111	1,152,578	11.93
TN Wesleyan	61,420	786,270	11.80
Tusculum	164,928	1,069,367	5.48
Union	76,077	688,795	8.05
U. of Charleston	82,860	1,178,137	13.22
U. of the South	133,458	1,059,802	6.94
Warren Wilson	78,051	1,107,309	13.19
WV Wesleyan	130,903	1,222,803	8.34
Wheeling	119,231	1,401,661	10.76
Total	**3,310,836**	**35,664,390**	**10.77**

About the Author

Alice Brown

Alice Brown graduated from Appalachian State University with a B.S. and M.A. in English and from the University of Kentucky with an Ed.D. in Higher Education. She taught in public high schools at Fort Bragg and Cary, NC, and in Richmond, KY. Her college teaching experiences include Appalachian State, Ohio University, Eastern KY University, and the University of KY. She worked in Special Programs at EKU and in Conferences and Institutes at UK and served as State Director for KY Elderhostel in both offices. From 1983 until 1993, she led the Appalachian College Program at UK (later named the Faculty Scholars Program), awarding fellowships to faculty at small private colleges in central Appalachia. That program grew into the Appalachian College Association, which she led for fifteen years, raising almost $50 million, $25 million of which was for endowment. This book covers her experiences during those years.

Since leaving the ACA in 2008 as president emerita, she has published, with Elizabeth Hayford, *How Boards Lead Small Colleges*,

Johns Hopkins U. Press, 2019, with funding for the research from the Spencer Foundation; *Staying the Course*, a book she wrote in 2013 about the thirty-five years Jim Taylor was president of the University of the Cumberlands; *Cautionary Tales: Strategy Lessons for Struggling Colleges*, Stylus Publishing, 2011; *Changing Course: Reinventing Colleges, Avoiding Closure*, with Sandra Ballard, Jossey-Bass, 2011. She also prepared a confidential report, *Seeking Clarity in the Briar Patch: The Almost Closing of Sweet Briar College*, 2015, on a grant from the Spencer Foundation. Since retiring, she has also published eleven articles, most in *Inside Higher Education*, and *The EvoLLLution*, and most recently she has produced a blog for American Association of University Professors (AAUP).

She has served on boards of the Skelly Foundation, the Southern Education Foundation, Colby-Sawyer College, HERS, Association of Collaborative Leadership, the Appalachian Studies Association and five other organizations. She has received six honorary degrees and six other awards, including Distinguished Alumnus of Appalachian State in 2010. As AWB & Associates, she has consulted with various universities and nonprofit organizations on fundraising and avoiding closure, including Lee University and Kansas Independent College Association.

Her husband, Harry, taught English at Eastern Kentucky University for roughly 40 years; her daughter Jennifer, a nurse, and her family live in Virginia; her son is a professor in Criminal Justice at the University of Texas, Rio Grande Valley. She has three grandkids: Murphy, Hugo and McKenzie—all three of whom are beautiful and brilliant. She looks forward to pointing them in the right direction when they are ready to select colleges to attend.